Catherine Howard

Catherine Howard

The adulterous wife of Henry VIII

DAVID LOADES

AMBERLEY

First published 2012

Amberley Publishing
The Hill, Stroud
Gloucestershire, GL5 4EP

www.amberley-books.com

Copyright © David Loades, 2012

The right of David Loades to be identified as
the Author of this work has been asserted in
accordance with the Copyrights, Designs and
Patents Act 1988.

ISBN 978 1 4456 0768 9
ebook ISBN 978 1 4456 1353 6

British Library Cataloguing in Publication Data.
A catalogue record for this book is available
from the British Library.

Typeset in 11pt on 17.6pt Palatino.
Typesetting and Origination by FonthillMedia.
Printed in the UK.

Contents

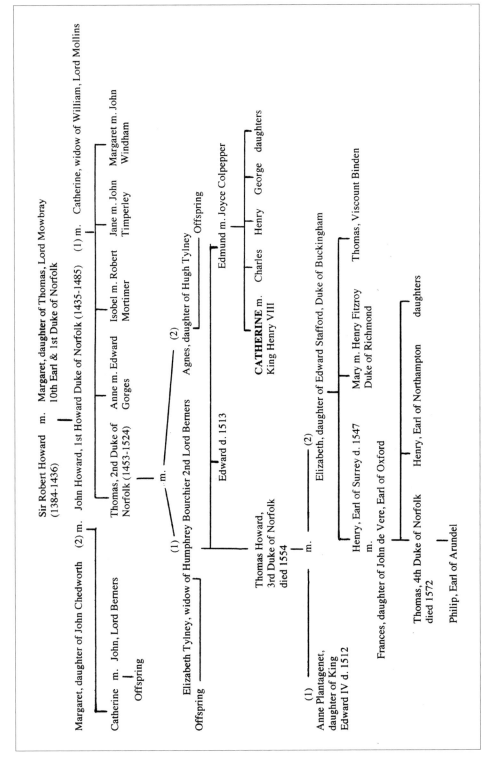

Genealogical Table of Catherine Howard.

Preface

Catherine has always been the odd one out among Henry VIII's wives. Anne Boleyn's misdemeanours were at the time, and have remained since, a subject for intensive speculation. The consensus of scholarly opinion now is that she was probably guilty of nothing worse than an incurable flirtatiousness, which exposed her to the attacks of politically motivated enemies. At the same time the king was guilty of a gullibility induced by the unstable nature of their relationship. Catherine Howard was different. In the first place she undoubtedly had a sexual past, which was concealed from the king when he married her; and in the second place her behaviour after their marriage gave every reason to suppose that she was an adulteress. Of all Henry's wives, she was the only one whose chastity could legitimately be called in question. She was very young and in a sense very innocent, but given the importance of the succession, and the need to be sure that any child borne by the queen was actually of the king's fathering, her relations with Dereham and Culpepper were sheer folly. Her marriage to Henry may have been sexually unsatisfying, but it was not tense, and the king was still rejoicing in his good and virtuous wife when the first news of her misbehaviour broke. The Howards had their enemies at court, but Catherine was not politically significant in the way which Anne had been. Rather she was the victim of the *mores* of a self-righteous husband, whose eye was constantly on the legitimacy of his offspring.

Catherine's political significance was circumstantial, and in order to understand her fate it is necessary to understand what kind of a monarch Henry was, particularly the intensely personal nature of his government. It is also necessary to understand how he had got to where he was in the summer of 1540; isolated in Europe by the politics of the royal supremacy, and at home by his decision to remove his trusted chief minister, Thomas Cromwell. The first had produced the disastrous Cleves marriage, from which he took Catherine on the rebound; and the second had opened the way for the ascendancy of the Howard family at court, of which Catherine was the symbol. She was only twenty when she died, and much about her childhood is obscure, so a biography is inevitably largely a study of her sexuality and its consequences. It must also be a study of the circumstances which raised her to the throne, and of the history of the succession issue. She has been the subject of numerous essays and speculative investigations, the most recent being the article in the *Oxford Dictionary of National Biography*. She was also given a chapter in my own *Tudor Queens of England* (2009). However the only full-length study remains that by Lacey Baldwin Smith, written over half a century ago (*A Tudor Tragedy*, 1961), and bearing all the marks of the period in which it was written. So the time has come to make another attempt at understanding this young lady and the times in which she lived, and I am grateful to Jonathan Reeve of Amberley Publishing for the suggestion that I should try.

I am also grateful to the Oxford University History Faculty for giving me an academic base, and the opportunity to attend many rewarding seminars; to the staff of Bodleian Library where much of the research was carried out; and to my wife, Judith for her unfailing sympathy and support.

DL

January 2012

Introduction: A King under God

Henry never had any doubts about his answerability to God, but he spent most of his life trying to find out what that meant. His father had reigned because God had given him the kingdom on the field of battle. His victory at Bosworth, and the consequent death of Richard III, had secured a title which in dynastic terms was distinctly fragile.[1] He had then married the daughter and heir of his predecessor, Edward IV, and that had served to reduce Yorkist sentiment to a dissident minority. The union of the roses of York and Lancaster was hailed by Tudor chroniclers as the ending of the disastrous feud which had divided the royal family over the previous thirty years, and gave Henry VIII an unassailable claim to the throne, but it did not tell him how he was to conduct himself as king. He was also keenly aware of the insecurity of life, having spent the first ten years of his life in the shadow of his brother Arthur who had died in 1502, leaving him as the sole heir, and in spite of this sudden change in his prospects his father had lived barely long enough to pass on his crown without any kind of a minority. His mother had died in 1503, and his brother Edmund in 1500, so he would have had no excuse not to be aware of the perils of mortality. God's power and his purposes were equally inscrutable.[2]

He spent the first few months of his reign trying to prove that God had been good to England in bringing to the throne such a glorious young man. Very conscious of his father's dour and somewhat mean image, he was determined to shine like the sun in splendour. The court was transformed, and the old king's financial enforcers, Sir Richard Empson and Edmund Dudley, went to the block.[3] He married and his young wife quickly became pregnant. Above all, he began to hanker for war with France, seeking to follow in the footsteps of his hero, Henry V. The nobility, long chilled by Henry VII's mistrust, were again in favour and looking to emulate their forebears in feats of arms. Unlike his father, Henry had no need to seek parliamentary endorsement of his title, because God had provided that. The old king had not believed that he was answerable to the Lords and Commons for the way in which he conducted his government, but recognition of his title at a time when it was liable to be challenged was valuable asset, representing as it did the consent and the allegiance of the realm.[4] He could not expect the universal adulation which followed his son's accession. When he needed money, beyond what the retrenchment of his existing revenues could achieve, he went to parliament to ask for it, and when he needed to alter the law, as he did over the keeping of retainers, he sought for the endorsement of that same body. He was more than a Chief Executive because he was answerable to no one, but he knew perfectly well that his power was not unlimited. He was a personal ruler, but he was a king under God and the law. What he thought his personal responsibility to God amounted to is not very clear, but he was orthodox and conventionally pious.

He was also careful not to transgress the law, but then he did not need to because the law as it then stood imposed very few restraints upon his freedom of action.[5]

Henry VIII was also a personal ruler, and much more obviously so. In the first place, with his education and sheer physical presence, he was much harder to overlook; but in the second place he also displayed a wilfulness which would have been quite alien to his father. He suddenly announced, to the astonishment of his council, that he had decided to wed his sister-in-law, Catherine of Aragon. Catherine had been lurking unhappily on the fringes of the court since Arthur's death, and Henry had at one point been betrothed to her. However that arrangement had been repudiated almost five years before, and Catherine had resorted to prayer in an effort to keep her hopes alive. Now suddenly came fulfilment; it is not surprising that Catherine was radiant, or that she believed that Henry was guided by the will of God.[6] He was quite happy to accept that belief also, and when his wife was delivered of a stillborn girl in January 1510, to dismiss that as any kind of portent of misfortune. Henry believed that he should be guided by his council, but that he himself should make all the relevant decisions. The role of the council was to advise, and to carry out the decisions once he had made them, but not to dictate. Policy, such as war and peace, were for him alone to determine. Consequently he got his war with France in 1512, led his army in person to the capture of Tournai in 1513, and spent the accumulated wealth which his father had bequeathed him, in spite of his council's reluctance to support him.[7] This was partly because he had by that time found a councillor after his own heart in the person of Thomas Wolsey. Wolsey had been introduced to the court by his then patron, Sir Richard Nanfan, at some time before 1507. He had become a chaplain to the king, and made the acquaintance of the Prince of Wales. When that prince became king in April 1509, he was well placed to exploit his friendship, and became the new king's almoner before the end of the year. By 1512 he was high in Henry's confidence, but it was when he was entrusted with the organisation of the Tournai campaign in 1513 that he really made his mark. He was rapidly promoted in the church, becoming Archbishop of York in 1514, and on Henry's insistence, a cardinal.[8] Wolsey had his own agenda, but it was totally devoted to enhancing the king's power, and when he became chancellor in December 1515 he used all his efforts to that end, particularly in extending the crown's equity jurisdiction through the Court of Star Chamber.

Wolsey was, as Henry VII had been, deeply suspicious of the traditional aristocracy, seeing in their culture of lineage a source of authority which was not dependent on the king for the time being. Consequently he set out to convince Henry that only personal service to himself should merit the rewards of creation and promotion. His great success in this campaign came in the case which he built up against the Duke of Buckingham in 1521. Buckingham was a proud man, who traced his ancestry back to King Edward III, and who regarded the king as a parvenu. By convincing Henry that he was guilty of treason, Wolsey won his point against the ancient nobility, and the king thereafter began to treat his aristocracy as a service group.[9] Apart from his own natural son, the creations which he made after 1525 were consistently for services to himself of a personal, military or administrative nature. In a sense Wolsey was too successful, and the king dismissed him in 1529, but in this respect the baton was picked up by his successor Thomas Cromwell, and by the end of his reign in 1547 the majority of Henry's peers were of his own creation, and their dependence upon him was not in doubt.[10] Nor was it only in this connection that Wolsey followed the policies of Henry VII. He encouraged the king to use the title of Majesty, rather than 'your Highness' or 'your Grace' in order to distance himself from his peers, whose culture of chivalry he in other respects accepted. He also encouraged Henry's appetite for lavish displays and entertainments, and lived himself in the grand style, because all such demonstrations of magnificence were for the king's honour. He was sometimes accused of running a rival court, but that was never his intention. Henry was, and had to be seen as, very much the centre of politics and patronage, and fortunately the king shared this view, retaining his personal control over policy throughout the period of the cardinal's ascendancy.[11] He might encourage his loyal servant to do the hard work which lay behind the scenes, but the critical decisions were his alone. Throughout the early years of his reign Henry deliberately set out to make the monarchy glorious and untouchable, and in spite of increasing financial stringency, he succeeded remarkably well. However, he also had to be accessible, not only through parliament but directly, and the court was open to a degree that must have given his security advisers nightmares.[12] Not only did the king go regularly on progress, he also went about much of his daily life in public, and was considered to be particularly amenable to petitions which were presented when he was returning from a hunting trip, or on his way to chapel to hear mass. Only the Privy Chamber was off-limits to petitioners, unless they could produce the substantial bribe which was necessary to engage the services of one of his gentlemen.

Only in one respect did Henry not live up to his magnificent image. He had no heir. His queen was nubile, and knew her duty, but the eagerly expected son did not come. There was a moment in January 1511 when Catherine was delivered of a boy, but the child lived only a matter of weeks and the rejoicings turned out to have been premature. There then followed a miscarriage and another stillbirth, and it was not until 1516 that the queen finally produced a child that lived, but that was a daughter and the problem was not solved.[13] Catherine was by then thirty-one, and was becoming worn down with successive pregnancies. She conceived only once more in 1518, and that resulted in another miscarriage. So Henry's magnificent physique turned out to be useless in the one respect in which it really mattered – the begetting of a son. Rather surprisingly in one so adept at the arts of courtly love, the king seems to have been faithful to his wife in the early years of their marriage. Apart from a somewhat problematic flirtation with Anne Hastings, the rumours of the king's 'amours' with which the court gossips kept themselves occupied were effectively without foundation. There were periods of stress in his marriage, most of all when Catherine's father, Ferdinand of Aragon, opted out of Henry's war with France in 1513, which the king saw as a betrayal. For a while there were reports that he would renounce his wife and seek pastures new, but these turned out to be without foundation, and if there was any gap in their co-habitation, it was over by 1515, when the queen became pregnant again.[14] Nevertheless, Henry was worried. It was the received wisdom of the time that such failures were always the woman's fault, and indeed there seems to have been nothing wrong with the king's sexuality at that point. It may have been to test this out that Henry took his first mistress, probably in 1517, when he became involved with Elizabeth (Bessie) Blount. In 1519 Bessie bore him an illegitimate son, whom he immediately acknowledged and named Henry Fitzroy; and having made his point, the king abandoned her to a marriage with Gilbert Tailboys, and began to look elsewhere.[15]

In 1520 the king was still sleeping with Catherine, and there is no sign that he had given up on her, but the fact that he took a second mistress indicates growing frustration. For how long, and how frequently, he shared his bed with Mary Boleyn is a matter for speculation, but she bore him no child, and whether that was by his will or hers remains uncertain. Another bastard would not have been much use to him, beyond demonstrating his continued potency, about which at this stage there seems to have been no doubt. Mary was given over to her husband, William Carey, at some time in 1525,[16] and it was undoubtedly sexual desire that drove Henry's pursuit of her sister Anne. However she held out on him, not being willing to become his mistress, and by the time that he proposed marriage to her in 1527, he was no longer sleeping with Catherine. So a period of prolonged abstinence seems to have followed, lasting until 1532, which casts some doubt on the king's sexual energy. By the time that she finally yielded to him, and became pregnant, he was over forty years of age; on the verge of old age by the standards of the time, and may well have found that his performance was deteriorating. Although he got her pregnant at least twice more during the three years of their marriage, there are indications that all was not well. At the time of her fall, in May 1536, Anne is alleged to have made disparaging remarks about the king's sexuality, which may have been invented, but which certainly aroused a particular fury in Henry, who may well have recognised their truth.[17] His second wife, like his first, had failed to provide him with the male heir which he so desperately needed, and that may well have played a crucial part in her disgrace. By 1537 he had two illegitimate daughters, neither of whom was capable of succeeding to the crown. The reasons why both of them were deemed illegitimate lie in the tangles of his married life, but even if either of them had been lawfully begotten, they would not have been satisfactory heirs. There was no Salic law in England, and so no reason why a king should not be succeeded by his daughter, but it was a most undesirable prospect. A princess was expected to marry, and was quite likely to marry into a foreign royal family, which raised the likelihood of a foreign king. Since there were large areas of government which were considered 'impertinent to women' this would mean that the queen's consort would hold the Crown Matrimonial and would be for many practical purposes the effective ruler. This was a deeply repugnant prospect, not only for Henry VIII but also for most of his subjects. Which is why they continued to support him through thick and thin in his pursuit of a satisfactory marriage.[18]

There were rumours of other 'amours' while Anne was still queen, and to which she is said to have reacted badly, but the only other woman in whom he was seriously interested was the one whom he married shortly after Anne's execution – Jane Seymour. Jane was no beauty, but she was obedient and submissive and that was what Henry's ego needed after bruising encounters with both Catherine and Anne.[19] A few months after their marriage, she duly became pregnant and in September 1537 produced the longed-for son, who was named Edward after his paternal great grandsire. Edward lived and flourished, but unfortunately his mother did neither. Within a fortnight of giving birth, Jane succumbed to puerperal fever, leaving Henry (for once) distraught. He now had his son, but had lost the means by which he had hoped to extend his nursery. The king was by this time forty-six years old, and the prospect of further offspring was receding by the year. His council, however, was insistent that he remarry, and bearing in mind the uncertainty of life in the sixteenth century, one can see why. Edward's life was too slender a thread upon which to hang the future of the English monarchy. There are, however, signs that the king's sexual energies were flagging. It took him over two years to find another bride, and she was found for him rather than being discovered by personal experience as the first three had been. This was a mistake, and he found Anne of Cleves so personally unappealing that he was unable to consummate their union. He found numerous excuses for this, and professed himself able to 'do the deed' with any other woman – but not with this one.[20] The result was an annulment on the ground of non-consummation, an outcome which provoked ribald amusement in the taverns of London, but nevertheless carried a serious message with it. Unless Henry could recover his libido, the prospect for further children, and consequently a secure dynasty, were remote. It would be no exaggeration to say that throughout the period from about 1510 until 1540, the king's sexuality was a political fact of the first importance, not only to himself, but also to his council and to the whole nation. A personal monarchy needed a secure succession, and that Henry had so far failed to provide. In 1500 his father had had three sons, but only one of them outlived him – what were the prospects for Edward? Catherine Howard's first task, therefore (and one for which she was exceptionally well equipped) was to encourage Henry to rediscover his sexuality.

The king had believed that God would provide him with a son, and in a sense he was justified, but it had cost him an immense struggle, both with his conscience and with the Church. When Edward was born in 1537, it was into a very different world from that in which Henry had set out to solve the problem of the succession about twelve years earlier. It is not surprising that the king's propagandists hailed his birth as God's vindication of all that had been done over the previous decade, because in truth Henry had redefined his relationship with the Almighty, and that in the most controversial manner. The canon law had always been accepted as a manifestation of the divine law, but in defying the pope Henry had broken that law, and consequently needed a new definition of the Law of God.[21] For most practical purposes this came to mean whatever the king said that it was, and Henry thus constituted himself as a unique intermediary between God and his people. However for certain purposes, and this involved the establishment of the royal supremacy, Henry invoked the alleged ancient traditions of his kingdom, and that meant proceeding by statute because parliament represented the will of the realm. Consequently the royal supremacy was declared (not created) by the Act in Restraint of Appeals and the Act of Supremacy, which effectively gave the king the right to represent the will of God in whatever way he chose.[22] In most respects Henry chose to be orthodox, and thus to see himself as a better Catholic than the pope, but when it came to authorising the English bible and dissolving the monasteries, he followed his own conscience (and interests) in defiance of the universal church. Henry never claimed to act as a priest or bishop (*potestas ordinis*), but he did claim the rights of ecclesiastical government (*potestas Jurisdictionis*), and appealed to his own status as an anointed king to justify this. The supremacy as thus created was personal to himself, and intended to be hereditary, but no provision was made for how it should be handled in the case of a child or a woman succeeding. Such circumstances had to be met by those in power at the time, and in the first instance led to the establishment of Protestantism, which

Henry himself would not have entertained.[23] During the king's lifetime, denial of the Supremacy became high treason, and thus welded God into the sanctions of the state. Henry undoubtedly believed that he had a 'hot line' to the Almighty, and thus that his position was sacred and unique. Acceptance of this situation was required of all those in public life, and so pervasive was the idea, that Catherine Howard at one point seems to have believed that he had supernatural access to the secrets of the confessional throughout his kingdom.[24] In the process of thus establishing himself Henry turned the English Church into a department of state, over which he was careful to exercise a detailed control, and reinforced that position with a thoroughgoing propaganda campaign, which lifted the monarchy into a kind of transcendent position, quite unknown to his predecessors who had been content to keep their Coronation oaths to defend the liberties of the Church. Henry might be held to have broken his Coronation oath by behaving in the way that he did, but woe betide anyone who tried to argue along those lines.

By 1540 Henry was thus a king by divine right, but he was also a king tied ever more closely to the laws and customs of his realm. To deny him his title of Supreme Head was a kind of blasphemy as well as high treason, but it was also an offence against the ancient constitution of England, at least as that was presented by the king's propaganda. To compensate for this, there was much emphasis on the duty of obedience. The burden of much teaching and preaching was that the prince was God's gift to the nation and must never be resisted, because it was upon him that the good order of the kingdom depended.[25] That good order was more than a matter of curbing lawlessness or religious dissent; it involved the whole structure of society. The divine law was the cement which held that entire edifice together, and the law which embraced the whole natural order. It decreed inequalities of wealth and status, the subordination of women to men, and of children to their parents. It decreed that a master might punish his servants, and a husband chastise his wife. Above all it decreed obedience to magistrates, and mainly to the chief magistrate, who was the king.[26] The positive law was an aspect of that divine order, and its adjustment from time to time by parliament a reflection of refinements in the will of God. It was an article of faith that parliament always legislated in accordance with the divine purpose, and that the ancient laws of England were expressive of that same purpose. Consequently obedience to the king was an act of religious commitment, because the king had the right not only to order the worship of the Church, but also to decree the succession to the crown. He had done that in the injunctions authorising the English bible, in the Act of Six Articles and in the Succession Acts of 1534 and 1536, and those who had refused to accept this congruence between statute and divine law had gone to the block or the fire.[27]

By the time that Henry married Catherine Howard in the summer of 1540, he was therefore carrying a lot of theoretical baggage, as well as the burden of his own sexuality. His repudiation of his previous marriage to Anne of Cleves depended upon his status as head of the Church, and his religious orthodoxy upon his own idiosyncratic interpretation of the scriptures. He was politically isolated in Europe and badly in need of a replenished nursery. A lot therefore depended upon the success of his fifth marriage.

1
The Much Married King

It is not entirely clear why Henry decided to marry Catherine of Aragon in June 1509. She had come to England in 1501 as the bride of Prince Arthur, after a long negotiation and several proxy weddings, but Arthur had died barely six months later, and it is by no means certain that their union was ever consummated.[1] He had been fifteen at the time of their marriage, and not in the best of health, while she had been seventeen. This placed them well within the canonical limits for cohabitation, and there is plenty of evidence that they slept together, but no evidence of anything further. As well as hopefully providing for the succession to the English crown, Catherine had been the symbol of an alliance between her father, Ferdinand of Aragon and King Henry VII, and as neither of them wished to give up that alliance, she was quickly betrothed to the king's surviving son, Henry, then aged eleven. However, for reasons connected with the death of Ferdinand's queen, Isabella, and the succession to the Kingdom of Castile, Henry abandoned his friendship with the King of Aragon, and in 1505 caused his son to repudiate his betrothal.[2] This was done when he reached his fourteenth birthday on the pretext that he had not been consulted, but the real reason was political. Although he made a fuss about the way in which she was treated, Ferdinand did not want Catherine back in Spain, confusing the succession issue, and Henry did not want to repay her dowry, so she stayed in England. The new Prince of Wales would thus have had abundant opportunities to get to know her as he grew up. In 1509 she was twenty-five, and King Henry VIII was just eighteen. She was apparently a very attractive young woman, still in the bloom of youth, while he was a magnificent specimen of manhood, very athletic and head and shoulders taller than his courtiers.[3]

They were, as everyone commented, a splendid looking couple, and it may have been simply that he fancied her. However, there could have been other reasons. In writing to Margaret of Savoy, the regent of the Low Countries, on 27 June 1509, Henry alleged that it had been in response to his father's dying wish.[4] This could have been so, because Henry VII had patched up his relations with Ferdinand since 1505, and the latter had actually used his daughter as an accredited diplomatic agent since 1507. On the other hand it could have been a polite fiction, designed to put a gloss of filial piety on what was essentially a selfish choice. At the same time, it could have been a calculated political move, because Henry was hankering after a war with France almost from the moment of his accession, and Ferdinand was an obvious ally. Eager and bellicose though he might have been, Henry was not so foolish as to believe that he could wage such a war unaided, and a marriage was the most obvious way of sealing a bond of mutual assistance. Ferdinand's relations with Louis XII had cooled noticeably over the last two years, and Henry's thinking was justified in 1511 by the speed with which Aragon signed up to Julius II's Holy League against Louis.[5] So the unromantic fact is that his marriage could have been part of his build-up to war, and a means of bypassing his council, which he knew was opposed to such a move. Most likely there were elements of all these factors in his decision, because it could not have been lightly taken. Not only were there numerous unresolved financial issues concerning the unpaid residue of Catherine's dowry, which had bogged down routine diplomacy between the countries for years, there was also the problem of the validity of such a union. It was well known that a marriage between a man and his deceased brother's widow was contrary to canon law, so that at the time of their first betrothal, in 1503, Pope Julius had issued a dispensation, which it was in his power to do. However, doubts remained and these were voiced in 1509 by William Warham, Archbishop of Canterbury. Was the dispensation valid? It had been based on the assumption that Catherine's marriage to Arthur had been consummated, but supposing it had not been? Did the dispensation cover the relationship which would then have existed?[6] In addition there may have been lurking at the back of some minds, although not apparently of Warham's (or Henry's), the thought that such a dispensation might have been *ultra vires*; beyond the pope's power, because the prohibition was based upon the word of God as expressed in the scriptures. There was therefore not only surprise, but a certain unease, when the king suddenly announced his decision to wed, within about five days of his father's death. Fuensalida, the Spanish ambassador, was so taken aback that he had to cancel plans which were already in hand for the princess's withdrawal to the Low Countries, and to start planning instead for the nuptials which took place in the Franciscan church at Greenwich on 11 June.[7]

Just eighteen days later Henry and Catherine came from Greenwich to the Tower of London in preparation for their joint Coronation. On 23 June they processed from the Tower to Westminster, and there on the following day they were crowned with great magnificence. 'For a surety,' wrote the chronicler Edward Hall, 'more rich nor more strange nor more curious works hath not been seen than were prepared against this coronation.'[8] There he swore to uphold the laws and customs of his realm, and received the allegiance of his assembled peers before proceeding to a gargantuan banquet which would have taxed the resources of anyone less youthful and exuberant. Catherine was ecstatic; not only had her prayers been answered, but she was sure of the firm friendship between her husband and her father. 'Among the many reasons that move me to love the king, my lord,' she wrote tactfully, 'the strongest is his filial love and obedience to Your Highness ... The news here is that these kingdoms ... are in great peace and entertain much love to the king my lord, and to me. Our time is spent in continual festival...' The last at least was no exaggeration; there was an almost unbroken round of revels, disguisings, pageants tilts and jousts, interspersed with long days in the saddle following hawks and hounds, and long nights dancing and making music.[9] Catherine meanwhile had serious business to attend to. The first was the negotiation of a formal treaty between her husband and her father which would be properly expressive of their mutual love and support; and the second was to beget an heir to the English throne. Paradoxically both matters came to a head at the same time, and within days of his being notified of the agreement of the treaty early in 1510, Ferdinand received a letter from his daughter informing him that she had been delivered of a stillborn girl. Assuming that this child had gone to its full term she must have become pregnant about a month after her marriage, which was promptly enough to be reassuring, even if the outcome had been disastrous. Neither she nor Henry appear to have taken this setback very seriously – a girl would have been only a token anyway – and within a few weeks, on 24 May, Ferdinand was informed that his daughter was again pregnant.[10] This time God would surely be good to them.

The following January this appeared to have been the case, when the queen was delivered of a son, who was named Henry and greeted with thunderous rejoicings. The king went to Walsingham to give thanks, and returned to Westminster to a splendid tournament and pageant. However, a few weeks later the young prince died in his cot, and joy was turned to lamentation. Both parents were devastated, and Catherine spent many hours in anxious prayer to discover what she had done wrong to deserve such grievous punishment. Henry rebounded more quickly, and began to preoccupy himself with his coming war.[11] In 1513 there were rumours that his marriage had broken down in the wake of this disappointment, but although there may have been tensions, that was not the case and early in 1514 Catherine again became pregnant. This appears to have gone to its full term, but in December she was delivered of another son, perhaps born dead, or perhaps living only a few hours. The queen again resorted to prayer, but Henry was by this time becoming seriously anxious. Three such misfortunes in a row argued something seriously amiss in his relationship with God, and after five years of married life, he still had no heir. These anxieties were partly relieved by the birth of Mary in February 1516, and the king became positively optimistic. The queen and he were still young, he declared, 'and by God's grace, the boys will follow'.[12] However, Catherine was by this time thirty, no longer young by the standards of the time, and was to endure only one more pregnancy in 1518, which resulted in yet another stillbirth. For a number of years thereafter she continued to grace the court, and to preside at its festivities, including those of the Field of Cloth of Gold in 1520, but there was to be no increase in the royal nursery. They were still sleeping together, and Catherine may have undergone an early menopause, but by 1525 it was fairly clear that she would bear no more children, alive or dead, and Henry in his mid-thirties, was faced with the prospect of having to pass his crown to a woman, which was an altogether unprecedented and hazardous situation.[13]

He did, however, have a son. Henry Fitzroy was born to his mistress, Bessie Blount in the summer of 1519. At just what point the king's eye began to rove in her direction is not clear; it may have been as early as 1514, but it seems clear that by 1517 Henry had two sexual partners, and by late in 1518 she had become pregnant. The birth of their son may have come as a great relief to Henry, who must surely have wondered whether his own inadequacies had not played a part in his wife's failure in that respect. The child was immediately acknowledged, and Cardinal Wolsey (who had already had to make similar arrangements for his own offspring), organised his fostering.[14] It seems clear that after her confinement, Henry had no further sexual relations with Bessie, and she was reabsorbed via her marriage to Gilbert Tailboys into that courtly context from which he had originally extracted her. It is by no means clear that the king ever had any intention of seeking to legitimate his son, but he made a gesture in that direction when he elevated him to the dukedoms of

Richmond and Somerset in the summer of 1525, to Catherine's bitter chagrin. Richmond was a royal title, and the child was immediately sent to 'preside' over the Council of the North, but that may have had more to do with Wolsey's agenda than Henry's.[15] By about 1522 the king had taken a new mistress in the person of Mary Boleyn, the elder daughter of his servant and diplomat Sir Thomas Boleyn. Mary and Henry slept together, intermittently at least, until about 1525, but she never became pregnant by him. This suggests some contraceptive knowledge on her part, because there is no reason to suspect the king's performance at this date, and she became pregnant quickly enough when she was passed on to her husband, William Carey, in the summer of that year. Their son, Henry, was born in March 1526.[16]

By that time the king was in hot pursuit of her younger sister, Anne. Anne had been brought up in the courts of Mechelin and Paris, and was considered more French than English in her demeanour and courtly skills. It was probably that polish which attracted Henry in the first place, because she was no great beauty. At some time in 1526 she apparently declined to become his mistress, and this focussed the king's mind on the state of his marriage. If he wanted a male heir, he would either have to legitimate Henry Fitzroy, or get rid of Catherine and start again. The first was too hazardous an option, and he began to consider ways of ending his union with Catherine.[17] Her behaviour had always been irreproachable, and divorce in the ordinary sense was out of the question, so it had to be a question of finding grounds for an annulment. These lay ready to hand in the fact of her earlier marriage to Arthur, the king's brother. The canonical impediments had been duly dispensed by Julius II in 1503, but supposing that dispensation was invalid? Henry focussed on that passage in the book of Leviticus which forbade a man from taking his brother's wife in marriage, and decided that he had broken the law of God. In the summer of 1527 he confronted Catherine with the information that they were not, and never had been, properly married, and a month or so later proposed marriage to Anne Boleyn. The queen's reaction was predictably tearful and outraged. How dare he suggest such a thing! More practically she realised that such a decision would have to be made in Rome, and promptly elicited the support of her nephew, Emperor Charles V, to make sure that no such verdict was ever passed there.[18] The wars in Italy had resulted in the sack of Rome by a mutinous Imperial army in March 1527, and when the news of Catherine's plight reached him, Clement VII was virtually a prisoner. However, neither the king nor Wolsey were able to take advantage of this situation. By the time that their emissaries reached him, the pope had recovered his equilibrium, and the emperor's influence was once again paramount in the curia.

Thus began Henry's six-year battle to get his first marriage annulled. The arguments and the envoys went backwards and forwards between London and Rome, as Wolsey struggled to overcome Imperial intransigence.[19] Early in 1529 he thought that he had won, when Lorenzo Campeggio was sent with a special commission to hear the king's case in England, but it soon transpired that he was deceived, and the collapse of the Legatine Court at Blackfriars in July signalled the end of his participation. Henry dismissed him from office, and relegated him to his see at York. Within a year he was dead.[20] While there was still any chance of his negotiations succeeding, Anne had been studiously polite to the cardinal, but when it became obvious that he had failed, she applied her unique influence over the king to the task of getting him dismissed, and turned instead to those who were beginning to favour a unilateral solution. This would involve repudiating the pope's jurisdiction in such a matter and turning instead to the authority of the Archbishop of Canterbury to reach a decision in England. There is some evidence that by 1530 Henry was coming round to such a view; the problem was, how to go about it? The first problem was that the incumbent archbishop, William Warham, was uncooperative. He had raised doubts about the validity of the king's marriage in the first place, and there is no reason to suppose that he had changed his mind, but such issues should be decided in Rome, not at Lambeth.[21] He was too old a royal servant to be openly obstructive, but his demeanour since 1527 had made it clear that he would not support the king's desire for an 'in house' solution to his problem. The second problem was that Henry had instructed his envoys in Rome to search the Vatican archives for evidence that the pope's spiritual jurisdiction did not extend to cases of matrimony, and of course they found none. In other words making distinctions between what the pope could and could not do was not going to work. By 1531 the king's intimate advisers were coming to the conclusion that if he wanted to annul his marriage, he would have to do it by rejecting the papal authority *in toto*, a situation for which they thought that they had discovered some precedent in the ancient annals of the kingdom.[22] The king was not yet convinced, and kept up his campaign in Rome, bullying the English Church into submission in order to demonstrate his power to do so. This may have been intended to blackmail the pope, or it may have been to prove to himself that the Church in England would not offer effective resistance if he did decide to go it alone. By 1532 his representations had made no noticeable progress, and Anne was still holding out on him, so that his frustration was both political and sexual – an explosive mixture.

Then in August 1532 William Warham died, and this event seems to have tipped the balance in the king's mind in favour of decisive action. In the summer of 1531 he had broken off relations with Catherine, dismissing her from the court and ending the *ménage a trois* which had prevailed since 1529, so he had been moving steadily in that direction, but Warham's death seems to have resolved his lingering uncertainties.[23] In September he created Anne Marquis of Pembroke in her own right, and in October took her with him on his long-planned visit to Francis I. This caused a mild embarrassment because Queen Eleanor refused to meet her on account of her ambiguous status; however Francis himself suffered from no such inhibitions, and when they met in Calais, they spent a long time in private conversation. This was good news for Henry because if he was to defy Imperial influence in Rome, he needed the support of the King of France, which Francis by this gesture appeared willing to grant.[24] After the meeting, the royal couple (as they may now be described) had been stormbound in Calais for a few days, and it was almost certainly during that time that Anne came to her critical decision. She was by this time sufficiently convinced of his intentions to yield to his importunities, and they slept together for the first time. There was clearly nothing amiss with the king's performance on this occasion, and by early January 1533 she was discovered to be pregnant. This forced the issue which had been in the air for so long, because if the child she was carrying was to be legitimate, Henry would have to marry her, and that meant taking whatever steps were available to end his existing union. Fortunately the vacancy at Canterbury meant that he was in a position to nominate his own man to the primatial see, and in fact had already done so.[25] Thomas Cranmer, Archdeacon of Taunton, was not the most obvious man for the job, but he did have the immense advantage of having already declared in the king's favour on the vexed issue of his marriage annulment. Until recently he had been an obscure Cambridge don, but more or less by chance had been given the opportunity to deliver an opinion to the king in which he represented the relevant decision as being theological rather than ecclesiastical, and had suggested canvassing the universities of Europe for favourable opinions on the issue; a suggestion which the king had taken up with alacrity.[26] Cranmer had been on a diplomatic mission in Germany when the decision was taken to summon him home and make him archbishop, a summons to which he responded, as he later claimed, with the greatest reluctance. He was consecrated on 30 March 1533.

Meanwhile Henry had quietly married Anne, and on 5 April Convocation broke the silence imposed by Rome on any discussion of the case, to declare that a marriage such as that of Henry and Catherine was impeded by a divine law which no pope could dispense. Parliament had already declared the archbishop competent to decide the case, and on 10 May he opened his court at Dunstable and did just that, declaring the king's first marriage invalid and his second good and proper.[27] On 1 June Anne was crowned as queen, and shortly after parliament tidied up the issue by forbidding any appeals to the Roman Court by subjects of the English crown. The outraged pope had simply been swept aside in a carefully organised coup, which had been manipulated by Henry's latest man of affairs, Thomas Cromwell. Cromwell had emerged from Wolsey's service after the latter's death in 1530, and his pragmatic political sense had quickly commended him to the king. He was essentially a 'ways and means' man who specialised in showing the king ways in which he could achieve his desired ends, rather than a decision maker, but that was what the king needed in 1533. The Act in Restraint of Appeals was largely his work, and the Act of Supremacy of the following year likewise.[28] By these two statutes and by his act of defiance, Henry had transformed his relations, not only with the Church but also with God. The Church was now a department of state, controlled by the king in parliament, and the king was directly dependent upon God, answerable to him alone for his policy decisions. In the process of carrying out this revolution, Henry had convinced himself that the papacy was merely a human institution, and like all human creations had become corrupt. He alone represented the gospel truth in its purity, which it was his duty to impose upon his subjects. He was a better Christian than Clement (who was in any case a simoniac), and was entitled to take his spiritual counsel where he thought best. If that meant listening to humanists and reformers, then that was clearly the will of God.[29] He took this responsibility with immense seriousness, and his later decisions, whether to authorise the English Bible, to dissolve the religious houses or to enact the conservative Six Articles of religion, have to be seen in that light. His actions may look self-serving, and financial in their motivation, but it must be realised that Henry was totally serious in his pretensions, and once he was convinced that the pope was a usurper, he saw himself as being primarily responsible for the spiritual well-being of his people. It was part of what it meant to be a king.[30] Some indications of this sense of responsibility can be seen in various actions and remarks going back to 1514, but it was only after 1532 that it emerged fully fledged onto the political scene.

Meanwhile Anne's pregnancy had reached its term, and on 7 September 1533 she was delivered of a healthy girl. The courts of Europe could scarcely contain their mirth. The King of England had moved heaven and earth for the sake of another daughter! The couple contained their disappointment as best they could, and the omens from a prompt pregnancy were good, but the fact remained that Henry had revolutionised his Church, and alienated the emperor, without producing the son that he clearly by now desperately needed. The child was named Elizabeth, and had a great future before her, but that was not anticipated in 1533, and when she was named as heir in 1534 it was more to distinguish her from her illegitimate half-sister than in any expectation of her succeeding to the crown.[31] Her parents' relationship did not suffer any immediate harm from her birth, but nevertheless over the next two years it became uneasy. Anne was politically very acute, and took her husband up on policy issues in a way which he thought unbecoming. She also took his wandering eye amiss, and indulged in tantrums of a kind which he had found fascinating during the long years of their courtship, but which were not appropriate to a wife who was supposed to be humble and submissive. Anne was anything but submissive, and never learned to behave as a sixteenth-century wife was expected to. Henry was very conservative in his expectations of wifely behaviour, and Anne did not conform. Their relationship, which was passionate and physical in its nature therefore became erratic, and when she miscarried of a second child in 1534, his demons began to return.[32] Early in 1536 a crisis was reached. Catherine of Aragon died in January, and the papal sentence which had ordered him to return to her was thus nullified, exposing Anne to repudiation in her turn. Then in February she miscarried of a son. There is no reason to suppose that there was anything wrong with the foetus, but the king was seriously alarmed. In what way could he have offended God a second time to be so deprived?[33] Anne had many political enemies, partly from the circumstances of her rise to power, and partly because of her close connections with France. There were therefore those who were disposed to take advantage of any doubts which the king may have had about his wife to bring about her downfall, and she gave hostages to fortune by a flirtatiousness which seems to have been second nature to her. In this connection a conversation with Sir Henry Norris on 30 April left itself wide open to misinterpretation, and Henry seems to have been suddenly convinced that she had been playing him false. Thomas Cromwell, by this time her arch-enemy, then worked on the king over the next few days to convince him of her adultery, and even persuaded him that his infatuation with her over so many years had been the result of witchcraft.[34] She was sent to the Tower and a comprehensive case was assembled against her, most of which consisted of inference and innuendo. She was even accused of incest with her brother, Lord Rochford, on no better grounds than that they had spent a lot of time together. However, implausible as the case may appear to modern eyes, only Henry had to be convinced, and that Cromwell succeeded in doing. She and her 'accomplices' were tried, convicted and executed; and before her death on 19 May her marriage to the king, which he had worked so hard to bring about, and which had been declared good by Cranmer less than three years before, was annulled by the same authority in a case which does the archbishop's reputation no good at all.[35]

It was thought at the time, and has been argued since, that one of the main reasons why Anne was hustled to the block, was that Henry was already enamoured of another young lady, by name Jane Seymour. Jane was the daughter of Sir John Seymour of Wulf Hall, near Marlborough, and had been around the court for a number of years, so the reason for the king's sudden infatuation is not very clear. However, he appears to have got to know her reasonably well during the last two or three months of Anne's life, and to have liked what he saw. In the first instance, she came of a good breeding stock. She was the fifth child, although the eldest daughter, of Sir John, with whom Henry had often joked about his celebrated virility, so the chances of her producing the much-needed son were obviously good. She was about twenty-seven in 1536, but her unmarried state seems to have had more to do with Sir John's inability to produce a suitable dowry rather than with any lack of attractiveness on her part.[36] Another point in her favour was that she had no political agenda, and unlike Anne, was docile and biddable. As Sir John Russell put it 'the king hath come out of hell into heaven, for the gentleness of this and the cursedness and unhappiness in the other'. Scarcely fair to Anne, but only to be expected in the circumstances. Anyway, Henry married her on 30 May 1536 with what was considered at the time to be indecent haste, and no doubt set about the task of getting her pregnant. Jane was not a party to the Lady Mary's surrender, which took place towards the end of July, but she quickly emerged as a good friend of that battered young lady. Mary was only about seven years younger than her stepmother, and her trouble arose from the fact that she had sided firmly with her mother, Queen

Catherine, during the protracted steps which led to the annulment of her marriage, a result which Mary refused to accept. Now that Catherine and Anne were both dead, the king turned his attention to her, and she was faced with the stark alternatives of surrender or trial for high treason. Urged and encouraged by Thomas Cromwell, she reluctantly surrendered, and was received back at court.[37] Jane quickly befriended her, and encouraged Henry to re-establish her household, which was done within a matter of weeks. In spite of its innocuous nature, the king's third marriage was not therefore without its political significance. The Seymour kindred was nothing like as aggressive as its Boleyn predecessor, but nevertheless the careers of her brothers prospered. Edward, already established in the Privy Chamber, became Viscount Beauchamp, and was sworn of the Council, while Thomas joined the select band of the king's intimates.[38] Sir John himself did not receive any preferment, but that may have been on account of his ill health because he died in December 1536.

In the autumn of 1536, while Henry was preoccupied with the Pilgrimage of Grace, or more likely out of relief that it was over in December, he succeeded in getting Jane pregnant. For this reason her much-talked-of Coronation was deferred, and although her condition developed normally, as the summer advanced the king became understandably jumpy. He even put off a planned visit to the north of England, not, as he pointed out, because Jane had asked for it, but out of enhanced sense of responsibility. What he could have done if anything had gone wrong is not entirely clear, but presumably his presence was thought to be an encouragement. Towards the end of September, the queen retreated into the customary female seclusion at Hampton Court, and went into labour on 10 October. After an easy pregnancy, the labour was long and bitter; anxiety mounted to fever pitch and public prayers were offered in London for her safe delivery. At length, however, on 12 October she was delivered of a son, and the child was alive and healthy. The relief and the rejoicings were unrestrained, not least on the part of the king himself. After twenty years of struggle and effort, the annulment of two marriages and the repudiation of papal authority, at last he had an heir!

> On St Edward's eve was born ... the noble imp prince Edward ... at the birth of this noble prince was great fires made throughout the whole realm and great joy made with thanksgiving to almighty God which hath sent so noble prince to succeed to the Crown of this realm.[39]

He was christened on 15 October with all the traditional splendour reserved for an heir to the throne, and his mother sat in the ante-chapel to receive congratulations. No one was surprised when Hugh Latimer, in a court sermon soon after, proclaimed that God was English, because Edward's birth was regarded as a vindication, not only of the king's sexual activity, but of all the policy decisions which had been made in England since 1530. Unfortunately, Jane did not survive to enjoy her triumph. By 18 October she had developed puerperal fever, and late on the 24th, she died. Henry's triumph had been bought at a high price, and he mourned her deeply, with a genuine grief which contrasted starkly with his reaction to the deaths of his first two wives. She was, as he expressed it, his first and only true wife, and now God had chosen to deprive him of her company. His council wasted no time in persuading him to remarry. Respectful as they may have been of his grief, they were only too conscious of the fact that the succession hung by the slender thread of one young life. A Duke of York (the traditional title of the king's second son) was not merely desirable but necessary, particularly after the experience of Prince Henry in 1511.[40] However, in contrast with his previous enthusiasm, the king was on this occasion reluctant. He may have been feeling his age (he was forty-seven), or he may have believed that there could never be another Jane. The search for a new wife began within a matter of months, and Henry must have sanctioned it, but it became an aspect of his foreign policy, not really connected to his personal feelings. He made a theoretical pass at the widowed Duchess of Milan, Christina of Denmark, but took her rejection of his advances with equanimity; and even made a half-jocular proposal to Francis I that a 'beauty parade' of French princesses be arranged, so that he could make his choice.[41] Eventually, in the autumn of 1539 he was persuaded to sign a treaty of alliance with Duke William of Cleves which committed him to a marriage with the duke's sister, Anne. This turned out to be a serious mistake, because his three previous marriages had been contracted on the basis of personal knowledge, going back in each case over several years, but in this case all he had to go by was a somewhat flattering portrait, and various personal descriptions by self-interested envoys who were anxious to persuade him. When he actually met the lady, he was seriously disappointed, and his famous libido seems to have failed completely. So much so that he was unable to consummate their union, and within few months was seeking an annulment on those grounds.[42] At this point Catherine Howard came on the scene.

Catherine was born at some time between 1518 and 1524, probably in 1522, as she was described (not very reliably) as being twenty at the time of her death. She was one of the five children with which Lord Edmund Howard's first wife, Jocasta Culpepper, presented him. Edmund was her second husband, and as she also had five children by her first union, Lord Edmund had some excuse for his straitened circumstances. Although he was the son and brother of a duke, his life before 1531 is extraordinarily obscure. In about 1510 he entered the Middle Temple, but seems never to have taken to the law, indeed in 1519 he was subjected to the royal wrath for having instigated a riot in Surrey. This was a scrape from which the Howard influence at court was able to extract him, but there is little sign of royal favour, even during the ascendancy of his cousin Anne Boleyn.[43]

Although he was approximately the same age as the king, he seems not to have shared his athletic tastes, and there is even some suggestion that Henry disliked him, although on what grounds is not known. The one thing that we do know about Lord Edmund is that he was constantly short of money, and that the royal bounty did not come to his assistance. He may have been bailed out from time to time by the duke, but the records are extremely sparse. His wife died in 1527, and as he still had a full nursery at that point he hastened to remarry, his second wife being Dorothy Troyes. Young Catherine was presumably brought up at home, and along with her earliest letters learned the necessity for piety and chastity in an aristocratic girl. It is not until 1531 that the position clarifies to some extent. In that year Edmund was appointed to the responsible, but not particularly lucrative post of Comptroller of Calais, and went off to take up residence in that town. His wife presumably went with him, but not the children. If Catherine was the youngest, the others were presumably of an age to shift for themselves, but she at the age of about eleven was placed with her father's stepmother, the Dowager Duchess Agnes, and there at Chesworth House near Horsham and at Norfolk House in Lambeth, she passed her adolescent years.[44] Her education was not neglected; she learned to read and write, and to speak passable French, but it was somewhat short of intellectual content, being stronger on decorum and courtly skills than on the things of the mind. She also learned to play the lute and the virginals, and it was that circumstance which led to her first downfall. In about 1536 her music teacher, Henry Mannox, took sexual advantage of his position. As she later confessed he touched her intimately, 'which became neither him to ask, nor me to concede', but apparently stopped short of full intercourse.[45] She was by that time about fourteen, and no doubt eager for the experience, her training in chastity not having been apparently pursued. The Dowager Duchess had a pretty good idea of what was going on, and boxed Catherine's ears when she found them in a compromising embrace. However she did not take the obvious step of dismissing Mannox, and he continued to pursue his quarry after the household moved to Lambeth, although it would seem with little further success.

This was probably due, not to any discovery of propriety on Catherine's part, but because he had been overtaken in her favour by Francis Dereham. Francis had been a Gentleman Pensioner to her uncle the third duke, and had only recently entered the dowager's service, but by 1538 he had secured sexual access to her young ward. Dereham and his colleague Edward Waldegrave were several times entertained by Catherine and her 'bedfellow' Kate Tylney in their bedchamber until the small hours of the morning, and this went on for a period of about three months.[46] Dereham addressed Catherine as his wife, and apparently used her in that sort. They exchanged presents and became sexual partners. The duchess was not ignorant of this, because Henry

Mannox in a fit of jealousy wrote to her anonymously, exposing the goings on in the girls' quarters, but she seems to have taken no action to prevent it. Because Dereham was of a suitable social status, she may have chosen to regard them as betrothed, in which case intercourse would have made a full marriage, but if that was her opinion then she kept quiet about it. Late in 1539 Catherine was selected as a maid of honour to Anne of Cleves, and Francis Dereham took himself off to Ireland. Meanwhile, in March 1539 Lord Edmund had died. During his eight years as Comptroller of Calais he may be constantly glimpsed going about his business, but without any sign that either his health or his fortunes were much improved. On one occasion he wrote to Lady Lisle, the Lord Deputy's wife to thank her for her remedy of the stone, as a result of taking which he had voided much gravel, not without pain.[47] However at another time he wrote that the remedy was worse than the disease, and it may well have been this complaint which carried him off at the not very advanced age of forty-eight. Only in marriage was Lord Edmund an unqualified success, each of his three wives bringing him lands and money which kept him afloat when he had no other visible means of support. The fees attached to the comptrollership were no doubt useful in this respect, but would not on their own have been sufficient to support the noble lifestyle to which he aspired. Catherine's reaction to his death is not known. It had been several years since they had lived together, and if any correspondence passed between them it has not survived. It may well be that she felt little grief; after all she now had an exciting new life to look forward to at the court – although how exciting that would turn out to be she could hardly have known.

2
The International Scene

The death of Catherine of Aragon in January 1536 wrought a slight but significant change in England's European position. The emperor's council had already warned him that his quarrel with Henry over his aunt's position was a personal matter which did not justify political action;[1] now that she was dead he was under no pressure to implement the papal sentence in her favour. He was also anxious to renew his war with France, and Henry, who had hitherto leaned to the French side, was a possible ally. This latest conflict had been provoked by the death of the childless Francesco Sforza on 1 November 1535, leaving a vacancy which Francis I felt that only he could fill. He proposed the transfer of the Duchy of Milan to his younger son, the Duke of Orleans, who would marry Charles's niece, Christina, and to add weight to his diplomacy invaded the neighbouring state of Piedmont-Savoy in January 1536. Piedmont was an ally of Charles, who became extremely angry over this act of aggression, so that, although it was intended as a limited operation, it became the trigger for a renewal of all-out war.[2] He tried to wean Pope Paul III away from his French alliance. The pope however, wanted peace. His

French association was not intended to extend to war, and he had no intention of changing sides. He had called a General Council to meet at Mantua in May 1537, and to stand any chance of success, that depended upon peace between the main powers, so Paul would devote all his efforts to preventing the kind of war upon which both the protagonists seemed set. Thwarted in Rome, the emperor turned his diplomatic attentions to London, and even urged Eustace Chapuys to be polite to Anne Boleyn in the hope of winning Henry's support. Thomas Cromwell was responsive, and Anne's Francophilia was one of the reasons he turned against her in May 1536.[3] However, her fall in that month and subsequent execution left the king in no mood for foreign adventures. He was primarily concerned to frustrate the Council of Mantua, because although he had appealed to such a council in 1533, when there appeared to be no chance of any such thing happening, now that it was a real prospect he became seriously alarmed. Clement VII, whose whole position was open to question, had been averse to the idea of a council, but Paul III suffered from no such inhibitions, and was anxious to deal in as authoritative a way as possible with the many problems afflicting the Church. One of these problems was the position of the King of England, and Henry rightly judged that no council convened by a pope would be likely to overturn a papal decision. He was insistent that his case be heard in a 'free' council, convened by the princes of Europe, and Mantua would clearly be no such thing.[4] It would be much better for it not to happen than for it to hand down a decision which he would, in theory, be bound to obey.

By June 1536, while Henry was busy dissolving the smaller religious houses and getting to know his new bride, Charles V was invading Provence. The French developed a 'scorched earth' policy and he was compelled to retreat. His northern army was repulsed at Peronne, and the Catalans refused to participate in an invasion across the Pyrenees, but Charles had no intention of giving up. He retreated to Italy and regrouped for a fresh assault. Meanwhile Francis had gone onto the offensive in the north-east, invading Flanders and Artois early in 1537. The campaign went backwards and forwards, but the Regent of the Netherlands, Mary of Hungary, was aware of deep discontents with the war within her jurisdiction, and of the dubious loyalty of several of the provinces. She agreed to talks with Francis, which resulted in the Truce of Bromy on 30 July 1537.[5] Charles was extremely angry with his sister for giving up in this fashion, because the French were now able to concentrate their forces in Italy where they speedily recovered the whole of Savoy, except for Nice. Henry, meanwhile, continued to do nothing. During the autumn he had been preoccupied with the Pilgrimage of Grace, which was followed by the Bigod rising in Yorkshire early in 1537, and he lacked both the will and the resources for an active foreign policy. He was satisfied that the ongoing war made the Council of Mantua an impossibility, and Paul postponed it *sine die* some months before it was due to convene.[6] Relations between England and the papacy showed no sign of improving, but at least he was spared the humiliation of having his appeal rejected. Thomas Cromwell was turning his attention to the major religious houses, which were beginning to surrender 'voluntarily', and although that promised to repair his finances in due course, such things take time, and he was by no means flush when the death of Jane in October 1537 gave a new twist to his international diplomacy.

His council was insistent that he should remarry, and very soon after Jane's death his ambassadors in France and the

Low Countries were instructed to begin making enquiries for a possible consort.[7] It is likely that this was done in the first instance without Henry's knowledge, because as we have seen, he was deeply sunk in grief, but by the beginning of 1538 he had awoken to the advantages of a foreign marriage. When Francis and Charles made peace, as they were bound to do sooner or later, the chances were that they would turn their attentions to schismatic England, and might act in concert if steps were not taken to prevent it. It was certain that the pope would seek to persuade them to such a course, and both would be anxious to gratify him. It did not matter very much which camp Henry chose to ally with, and his first preference seems to have been for France. Early in 1538 Sir Peter Mewtas of the Privy Chamber was sent across to assess the attractions of Marie, the daughter of the Duke of Guise, but before he arrived in February Marie was contracted to James V of Scotland, and married him in early May.[8] Intentionally or not, Scottish diplomacy had been too swift for him. Shrugging off his disappointment (if he felt any) Henry next turned his attention to Christina, the niece of Charles V and the recently widowed Duchess of Milan, and sent Sir Philip Hoby over to inspect her. With Hoby went Hans Holbein, and it is upon the rapid sketches made in the course of this visit that the famous portrait was based.[9] In the spring of 1538 Henry's matrimonial plans, or those being canvassed in his name, became luxuriant. A double marriage was proposed; of Henry with Christina, and of his daughter Mary, then aged twenty-two, with the brother of the King of Portugal, Dom Luis. At the same time the king was discussing a whole range of betrothals with the French ambassador, including Edward, then aged a few months, with the emperor's daughter, and Elizabeth, aged five, with a son of Ferdinand, King of Hungary.[10] How seriously any of these proposals were taken is not clear, but Henry does seem to have been in earnest about the Duchess of Milan. There were, however, various snags; the king wanted a sight of her; and they were close enough in kindred to require a dispensation. This presented no problems to the emperor, but Henry did not recognise the pope's jurisdiction, and would accept no order from him. Moreover, Christina herself was reluctant to become Henry's fourth wife 'for her council suspecteth that her great aunt was poisoned, that the second was put to death, and the third lost for the lack of keeping of her childbed…'[11] At the end of the day, there was no overcoming these objections and the project lapsed.

By May 1538, moreover, the French had come up with new proposals. What about Louise, Marie of Guise's sister, or Renee, a third girl of the same house? There was also Marie of Vendome, Anne of Lorraine, or Francis's sister, Margaret. By midsummer Henry was toying with no fewer than five suggestions, and negotiating a match for Mary with Charles de Valois.[12] All these complex negotiations, and this lurching to and fro between the Valois and Habsburg camps were designed at least as much to protect England's international interests as to provide a bride for the king, and in the event they were more successful in the former context than they were in the latter. Both sides were becoming financially exhausted by the protracted war, and in June 1538 Francis and Charles met at Nice, and with papal mediation, negotiated a ten-year truce. Paul was jubilant. At last the circumstances seemed right to issue the bull of excommunication which he had prepared against Henry three years earlier, and on 17 December such a bull was promulgated, absolving the king's subjects of their allegiance and deposing him in the interests of his (lawful) daughter, Mary.[13] On 12 January 1539 the French king and the emperor finally concluded a peace, in which each promised not to enter any new agreement with England without the other's consent. There was talk of withdrawing their ambassadors, and it seemed that the long-awaited crusade was about to begin.

Henry thought so at any rate. He ordered musters right across the south of England, and put defence works in hand at Calais and Guisnes. The Scottish border was fortified, and ships forbidden to leave English ports without a special royal licence. It seemed that a triple attack was impending, from France, the Low Countries and Scotland, James V having been brought into the Continental alliance by his marriage with Marie of Guise. The king's great ships had been repaired and rebuilt over the previous three years, and he now mobilised them, putting them on standby in the Thames and at Portsmouth to sail against any invasion fleet.[14] Above all, he decided to fortify the South Coast, and blockhouses were hastily thrown up from Pendennis to Hastings, very often using the stone from dissolved monasteries These were armed with cannon drawn from the royal armouries, and Henry ordered extra guns from the founders to equip them.[15] South-east England was in a frenzy of preparation. Ditches were dug, ramparts and palisades thrown up and munitions collected. Alarming reports spoke of a fleet gathering at Antwerp and of an army mustering in Flanders. The king toured the coastal defences and inspected his navy at Portsmouth. On 8 May he reviewed the musters at St James's Park. Meanwhile Reginald Pole, that bird of ill omen, had arrived in Spain on the first stage of his mission to motivate Charles and Francis to the attack, which was generally expected.[16] Edmund Bonner and Thomas Wyatt, ambassadors with France and the Empire respectively, were instructed to prise apart this unlikely alliance, using their best endeavours to this end. In theory England was in the greatest peril, and if there had been any stirring of rebellion, or if Reginald Pole had had ships and men at his command, Henry might well have been overthrown. However, if there was one thing which was designed to rally Englishmen behind their king, it was the prospect of foreign intervention against him, and in 1539 there was no sign of the discontent which had nearly paralysed the country three years earlier. Moreover Pole's mission was a failure. He had an interview with Charles and found him quite unwilling to take any action against Henry. The Turks and the Lutherans were giving him enough trouble without adding to his list of enemies. He did not rebuff the cardinal totally, but told him that any action on his part would depend upon Francis moving first, knowing perfectly well that the French would make the same condition. So it turned out, and although Pole put a brave face upon it, telling Francis that the emperor was willing, he was advised not to enter France, and retired to the papal city of Carpenteras to await further instructions.[17] When these arrived in August, they ordered him to return to Rome.

As 1539 advanced it became apparent that the invasion scare was a false alarm. As early as March Francis sent a fresh ambassador to England, and in April wrote to Henry assuring him that the warlike preparations which were visible in Picardy were aimed against the emperor and not against him. In other words the Treaty of Toledo, although only three months old, was already on the point of breaking down. Although intervention by the emperor remained a remote possibility, it was clear that the French would not join him, and by July the immediate crisis was past. Meanwhile, however, the alarm had generated a diplomatic initiative of an altogether unexpected kind, because in January Christopher Mont had been sent to the Duke of Saxony and the Landgrave of Hesse, indicating Henry's willingness to join the League of Schmalkalden.[18] At the same time feelers were put out to Christian of Denmark with a similar end in view; to end the king's diplomatic isolation and to attract allies against the expected papal assault. Christian responded doubtfully, expressing a willingness to join with Saxony and Hesse to form an alliance at some time in the future, should the Germans be so inclined. The Germans were not so inclined. They responded very coolly, shrugging off Henry's warnings of Imperial betrayal and saying that they could see no point in sending a mission to England, which had rejected their overtures in the past.[19] They did eventually send a small and undistinguished embassy which reached England in April, and which achieved nothing. This was partly because the Lutheran princes had come to terms with the emperor at the Imperial Diet, and partly because Henry felt it incumbent upon him to clarify his doctrinal position, which he did in the conservative Act of Six Articles, which was passed on 2 June. This made any agreement with the League impossible, and the Lutheran delegation went home. Henry's need for allies was by that time less urgent, but it had not gone away, and soon became entangled in his search for a wife, both the French and Imperial options being apparently ruled out because of the political circumstances.

The possibility of a link with the Duchy of Cleves had been raised as early as June 1538, when it was somewhat vaguely suggested that Mary might marry a son of the duke and Henry a kinswoman, but at that time it had been buried in the pile of other proposals being considered. It was resurrected in January 1539, when Christopher Mont's instructions included the sounding out of the Schmalkaldic princes about the desirability of such marriages, and making some enquiries about the duke's eldest daughter, Anne.[20] Anxious perhaps not to appear totally negative in their response to Henry, the duke and the landgrave expressed themselves enthusiastic, although it was not up to them to make the offer. Some six weeks later a three-man embassy led by Edward Carne was sent to the Duke of Cleves. By that time William had succeeded his father, who died in February, but he was equally interested in the proposal. William was not a Lutheran, but might roughly be described as a Christian humanist, very similar in his doctrinal position to that taken by the King of England. However he was not a papalist and was at loggerheads with the emperor over the Duchy of Gelderland, which had been inherited by his father in July 1538.[21] He was linked to the Lutheran princes by the marriage of one of his sisters to the Elector of Saxony, which added to his credentials as an opponent of the emperor, and (equally important) he was able to supply the mercenary soldiers of which Henry felt such a need at that time. Carne too heard good reports of Anne, and in any case was anxious to make a success of his mission. Duke William, however, proved hard to pin down. He seems to have enjoyed having the King of England supplicating for his favours, and made difficulties about providing a portrait of Anne for Henry's information. Only an old picture was available, and when Carne asked to be allowed to compare this with the original, the Chancellor of Cleves was evasive. There was also the little matter of Anne's pre-contract to the Duke of Lorraine. 'The further we go, the more delays' as Carne despondently reported.[22]

Henry was becoming impatient, and in early July sent another envoy, William Petre, to hurry things along. This was soon followed up by the despatch of Hans Holbein, with strict instructions to paint not only Anne but also her sister Amelia. Apparently impressed by Henry's pertinacity, the duke placed no obstacles in his way, and by 11 August Holbein had completed his mission. At the end of the month he returned to England, and presented his efforts to the king. This portrait of Anne, which now hangs in Victoria and Albert Museum, was only too successful in whetting Henry's appetite, and seems to have created a false expectation which was to be cruelly disappointed when he actually met her.[23] Satisfied at last that the king's intentions were honourable, on 4 September Duke William commissioned an embassy to come to England and negotiate a treaty of friendship and marriage. It arrived on the 24th, and having satisfied themselves that it was actually Anne and not Amelia that Henry was interested in, they dismissed her pre-contract as a matter of no importance. The marriage treaty was concluded on 6 October. Once he was convinced of the king's seriousness, the duke placed no further obstacles in his way, and a last minute attempt by the Count Palatine to revive the case for the Duchess of Milan was simply brushed aside.[24] The Count Palatine was the husband of Christina's sister, and was trying to press her claim to the throne of Denmark. He was anxious to enlist Henry's support for such a claim, but the king (quite rightly) was not interested. Word of this success was quickly conveyed to Cleves, and the preparations for Anne's journey commenced. She may well have been somewhat daunted by the prospect, because she had been brought up to be the bride of a minor German princeling, not to preside over a grand and sophisticated court. In the first place she spoke no language other than her native Low German, and knew no dances save those of her homeland. In the domestic skills appropriate to a noble wife she was well seen, but of intellectual interests she had none at all. Those who knew her might have warned Henry of what he was in for, but they lacked the contacts to do so, and the English envoys, who must have suspected as much were too concerned to bring about the marriage to seek such difficulties.[25]

Meanwhile, about 7 November, Anne set off from Dusseldorf on her journey, travelling in a gilded chariot and nobly, indeed royally escorted. So large was her entourage that it sometimes covered as little as five miles in a day. When she reached Antwerp on 4 December the citizens gave her the warmest of welcomes, and she was accommodated in the House of the English Merchants, the Merchant Adventurers, who no doubt hoped to make a goodly profit out of the king's new German alliance.[26] In theory this whole journey to the coast, which involved both Imperial and French safe-conducts, was paid for by the Duke of Cleves, but in practice most of the expense was met by Henry, who also forbore to ask for the payment of the 100,000 gold florins (about £18,000) which should have accompanied her as dowry. This payment was included in the treaty for the sake of the duke's honour, but the king privately agreed to waive it. Including the trumpeters loaned by the emperor, the train which was to accompany her to England numbered 263 persons, of whom it was intended that eighty-eight should remain in attendance on the queen after her wedding.[27] Going by way of Gravelines, she reached Calais on 11 December where she was warmly received by the Lord Deputy, Lord Lisle and his wife. In spite of the language difficulty they were favourably impressed by her, and judged that her sweet nature would make her an easy mistress to serve. They taught her some English card games, and gave her some tips on the etiquette of the English court, lessons of which she was very much in need.[28] Anne had plenty of time to indulge in these lessons, as she was stormbound in Calais for over a fortnight, whist Henry waited, and kept a solitary Christmas at Greenwich. On the 27th she crossed at last to Deal, with the king's ships providing an honourable escort, and proceeded via Dover and Canterbury to Rochester, where she arrived on New Year's Day, 1540.

Meanwhile, Henry decided to try a little old-fashioned knight errantry. He was in any case consumed with curiosity to see this paragon of whom he had heard so much, and decided to intercept her incognito.[29] He consequently gained admission to the bishop's palace where she was staying, and burst in upon her unannounced. The poor girl was completed fazed by these tactics, and apparently thought that she was about to be kidnapped. It might have occurred to her that nobody less than the king could have so penetrated the security by which she was surrounded, but such a thought does not seem to have occurred to her. In these circumstances her lack of English was an additional handicap, and she was left completely tongue tied. Henry, who was expecting the kind of witty response which he would have got from Catherine or Anne Boleyn, was bitterly disappointed. He withdrew with his companions, and after a suitable interval reappeared in his own person, properly heralded. She abased herself and they exchanged formal greetings whereupon he departed, leaving the New Year gift which he had brought for her to be delivered by a companion the following morning. Not only her demeanour but also her appearance had been unsatisfactory. He had apparently been expecting a beauty, and what confronted him was this rather plain and dumpy German girl, who could not think of anything clever to say in any language. 'I am ashamed that men have so praised her as they have done and I like her not' was his verdict upon their encounter.[30] He declared his discontent to Cromwell, who had masterminded most of the negotiations, saying that if he had known the truth about her she would never have come to England.

On 2 January she reached Greenwich, and was received with all due honour. The wedding was supposed to take place the following day, but Henry was by this time desperate to escape from his commitment and tried unsuccessfully to raise the issue of her pre-contract. There was no way out and they were duly married at Greenwich on 6 January. The international situation dictated it, even if personal inclinations did not, because the last thing Henry could afford to do at that particular moment was to upset his friendship with the Duke of Cleves. The emperor had decided to demonstrate his friendship with the King of France by returning overland from Spain to Germany, passing through Francis's dominions, and was actually being entertained in Paris on the day in question.[31] There could have been no better demonstration of Henry's potential isolation in Europe than this display of togetherness, and the king realised that perfectly well. 'My lord,' he is alleged to have told Cromwell, 'if it were not to satisfy the world and my realm, I would not do that I must do this day for none earthly thing.' In these unpromising circumstances it is not surprising that their wedding night was a fiasco. Henry found fault with her appearance, and even doubted that she was a virgin, and she for all her twenty-five years, was so innocent that she did not know what was supposed to happen on a wedding night. By that time her English household was in place, and as she struggled to communicate with her ladies the following morning, they realised with mounting incredulity that she had no idea what consummation meant. Henry had been very polite, and had kissed her nicely – need there be more?[32] Lady Jane Rochford must have spoken for them all when she said that at this rate it would be long time before a Duke of York appeared. For a while Henry persisted in sleeping with her, but more for form's sake than because he had any desire to 'do the deed' with her. He remained scrupulously courteous, and she appeared in public as the queen, being everywhere received as such. Her jointure was put in place, lands worth more than £3,000 a year being allocated for that purpose. No one would have gathered that there was anything wrong, but beneath the surface, feet were paddling hard. After Easter, by which time Charles's entertainment in France had ended and frost was again beginning to penetrate their relationship, Henry was discovering scruples about his fourth marriage. It was, he decided, invalid for two reasons; first because he had not consented to it, which was witnessed by his failure to consummate it; and secondly because Anne was not competent to consent on account of her previous betrothal to the Duke of Lorraine.[33] The second cause was well known, and had been dismissed as an obstacle in the course of the negotiations. The pre-contact had taken place, but it had been renounced formally as far back as 1535. The only point of substance in this objection was that documentation proving the renunciation had been requested of the council in Cleves at the time of the treaty but had never in fact been received. When the ambassadors from Cleves were summoned and informed of this fact they expressed astonishment, and offered to send for copies.[34] To make the matter sure, Cromwell caused Anne herself to renounce the contract with Lorraine, and that itself should have settled the issue. However, that was not what the king wanted, and he began to mutter about not being 'well handled'. Moreover when the documents did arrive from Cleves, it transpired that there was a doubt as to whether the contract had been entered into *per verba de futuro* or *per verba de praesenti*. In the former case Anne's renunciation would have been sufficient to end the matter, but not in the latter.[35]

The doubt was sufficient, together with the fact of non-consummation, for the king to take the matter to Convocation. Anne was packed off to Richmond on the pretext that there was plague in London, and Cromwell caused parliament to petition the king to investigate the circumstances of his marriage, listing the causes allegedly impeaching it. On 7 July Convocation was commissioned under the great seal to commence proceedings, and two days later its decision was signed and sealed. Henry was not, and never had been, married to Anne of Cleves.[36] Parliament swiftly confirmed this, and messengers were sent to Richmond to convey the tidings to Anne. To everyone's surprise, she proved to be absolutely submissive, and it may well be that the news came as a relief to her. No longer would she be called upon to endure the nightly charade of the royal bedroom or pretend to be a royal consort. She confirmed that their union had never been consummated (it having been explained to her what that meant), and dutifully wrote to Henry, addressing him as 'brother'. It may well have been to evade subsequent pressure on her to marry in Germany, that she decided to stay in England, accepting the status of 'sister' which was offered her. In his own relief at her acquiescence, the king was generous, giving her two houses, a sizeable household and £500 a year.[37] Most of her

English household were stood down, but those servants who had accompanied her from Germany (such as wished) were allowed to remain. Despite her ignorance of the language and of English ways, which had been only partly removed during her six months as queen, she settled down on the fringes of the court, where she remained an occasional but welcome guest. She never married, and died in 1557. Her real bother, the duke, was disconcerted by these developments and would have preferred her to return home, but was not disposed to make a fuss. After all, if Anne accepted her dismissal so easily, there was little reason for him to object, and formally at least, his friendship with England remained intact, if increasingly irrelevant.[38]

So why was Henry enveigled into this marriage in the first place? The collapse of his negotiations with the Schmalkaldic League, and his urgent need for a Continental ally, must have been the prime causes. But why Anne? She was available and apparently willing, and the king had heard good reports of her. However, the fact was that these reports had been mostly second-hand, and they had been filtered by Cromwell. Less flattering descriptions were not allowed to reach the king's eyes, particularly a caution by Nicholas Wotton, written in May 1539, which described her as uneducated, unmusical, and spending all her time sewing. 'For they take it here in Germany for a rebuke and an occasion of lightness that great ladies should be learned or have any knowledge of music...'[39] His warning went unheeded. The part played by Holbein's portrait in his deception has probably been overestimated. It was apparently a good likeness, and it came on the scene fairly late in the negotiations, but what it shows is a face lacking in all animation, and uncomfortably surrounded by gorgeous apparel. That Cromwell deliberately misled his royal master is equally unlikely, in spite of his selective use of the reports. He was keen on the union, and pushed it in all the ways that he could, but all the critical decisions were made by the king. Eventually it was Henry himself who decided to bring her to England, and anything else is pure self-deception. Moreover, once Cromwell was convinced of the king's aversion to her, he set about dissolving the marriage with his customary efficiency.[40] The link between the annulment and his fall, which took place at the same time, is more apparent than real. Anne was completely out of her depth in her dealings with Henry, and had no idea how to please him. In the words of one historian, she was 'an unawakened girl, lacking both charm and fire', but the mistake was Henry's, and his alone.

3
Domestic Politics

The 1530s were Thomas Cromwell's decade, the period during which this brilliant and manipulative operator showed Henry the way to achieve objectives which were desired but apparently out of reach. He was an arch-facilitator, and so influential that it is sometimes even now difficult to determine which were the king's ideas and which were his own.[1] In 1540, however, he overreached himself, and his fall and execution marked the end of a period of innovation and experiment in royal policy, a piece of punctuation which was accompanied almost simultaneously by the rejection of Anne of Cleves and by the Howard marriage. Henry, it seemed, was rejecting the path of evangelical reform which Cromwell had been anxious to pursue, and was looking instead to the conservative Howard clan to provide him with the comfort and support which he needed in his increasingly lonely eminence.

Cromwell was a self-made man. Born in about 1485, he was the youngest son of a Putney innkeeper called Walter Cromwell, with whom he fell out as an adolescent. Being an independent-minded youth, he then took himself off to the

Continent. There he wandered through the Netherlands, France and Italy, supporting himself as best he could.[2] Part of the time at least, he seems to have served as a soldier, and is alleged to have fought in the French army at the Battle of Garigliano in 1503. Thereafter he turned to trade, and managed to persuade a Venetian merchant to take him into his service. He remained in Italy for several years, no doubt undertaking journeys on his master's behalf, and in 1513 stayed briefly at the English Hospice in Rome. He then returned to the north, and in some way managed to secure the credit which enabled him to deal on his own behalf in the great mercantile capital of Antwerp. In 1514 he came back to London, married and embarked upon a career as a lawyer, although where he acquired his training for such an enterprise is not known. In 1516, when he was thirty-one, he entered the service of Cardinal Wolsey, who was famous as a spotter of talent, and presumably continued his self-education in the law.[3] He also became friends with Alderman John Robinson of Boston, Lincolnshire, and in 1517 and 1518 undertook two missions to Rome to obtain a Bull of Indulgence from Pope Leo X in favour of a guild which Robinson had founded in that town. As happened with Martin Luther a little earlier, the experience is supposed to have put him off the curia for life. His only benefit from the journeys (according to John Foxe) was that they enabled him to learn large sections of the New Testament by heart.[4] By 1520 he was well established as a lawyer in Wolsey's entourage, undertaking cases in Star Chamber as well as in the courts of Common Law, and apparently continuing his private practice in the latter as well. By 1522 he was described as 'gentleman' in a power of attorney, and in 1524 became a member of Gray's Inn, which marks his acceptance by the legal establishment.[5] In spite of his ruffianly youth, which he freely confessed, by 1525 the innkeeper's son from Putney had arrived in the ranks of the elite. In 1523 he was provided a seat in the House of Commons, and made an impressive speech, possibly instigated by Wolsey, urging the king to make proper provision for the defence of the border against Scotland before embarking on any campaign in France. This speech did not change the king's policy, but it did indicate an orator with a penetrating view of political reality. At the same time he became one of the cardinal's most trusted councillors, and his right-hand man in the dissolution of those small religious houses whose endowments were earmarked for the educational foundations in Oxford and Ipswich.[6]

And then in the autumn of 1529 Wolsey fell from power, scattering his servants in all directions. Cromwell, however, was not among them. His first reaction to the news was a mixture of disbelief and despair, because it seemed that all that he had worked for and achieved had been ruined. He remained in the cardinal's service until the end, advising him about the winding-down of his extensive commitments, and protecting him from an attempted Bill of Attainder in the parliament which met in November 1529, and in which he had managed to secure a seat for the borough of Taunton, which was still in Wolsey's gift as Bishop of Winchester.[7] It seems to have been Cromwell's devotion to his master which first attracted the king's favourable attention, because he appreciated such loyalty, as well as recognising his talents. The cardinal died in November 1530, and by early 1531, Thomas was in the service of the king. Later in that year he was already being referred to as a councillor, and although the term may have meant no more than specialist legal advisor, it certainly indicated that he had quickly arrived at a position of confidence and favour. By the end of 1532 he was recognised as a leading adviser to the king, with a special brief for handling his affairs in parliament. His victory in this connection was probably signalled in the acceptance by Convocation of the principal that the law of the church would henceforth depend, like the secular law, upon the assent of the monarch.[8] This directly foreshadowed the Act in Restraint of Appeals of 1533, which first cut the jurisdictional links between England and Rome, and enabled the decision of the archbishop's court upon the king's tangled matrimonial affairs to be regarded as final. It is probably true to say that although the motivation for these developments came from Henry, Cromwell had a much clearer view of the royal supremacy and its implications than did the king. They were to spend the next seven years working out those implications, but it was Cromwell's clear and realistic vision which placed him in the role of tutor, a role which he eventually presumed upon a shade too far.

Just as he had been devoted to the cardinal's service while that was relevant, so he now became dedicated to the king's. Wolsey had been concerned to increase the central authority of the government, and he had convinced Henry of the need to do this. The king's aspirations, however, remained unfocussed, and it was Cromwell who turned them into a programme of administrative and political reform. This concentrated almost from the start on the role of parliament, because he perceived a qualitative difference between the prerogative authority of the crown, and the power of the king in parliament, which symbolised and in a sense represented the consent of the realm.[9] It was already recognised that only the parliament could approve direct taxation or make new law, and Cromwell built on this position, using it to secure the dissolution of the king's first marriage and the erection of the royal supremacy, a development which involved the creation of a theory of national sovereignty, which built upon, but far transcended, the king's earlier expressed views of the nature of his authority.

> Where by divers sundry old authentic histories and chronicles it is manifestly declared and expressed that this realm of England is an Empire, and so hath been accepted in the world, governed by one supreme head and king...[10]

And the Church was embraced within that jurisdiction. From there it was a conceptually easy step to settle the succession by way of statute, to arrange that First Fruits and tenths should be paid to the crown, and to abolish those long-standing nuisances, the legal franchises. The Marcher lordships of Wales were done away with, and the king's writ ran uniformly throughout the land.[11] This reliance on statute called for careful management, not only of the draft bills but also of the composition of the House of Commons. The king could lean effectively on the House of Lords, but it was up to Cromwell to secure the necessary majorities in the Lower House, using the resources of royal patronage and his own extensive networks to secure the return of tractable members. It would be an exaggeration to claim that he packed the House, he did not have the resources to do that, but he certainly managed to place enough officials and other suitable men to take initiatives which the other members would follow.

All this required a great deal of work, and Cromwell was indefatigably industrious; not only in the manipulation of elections, but also in managing the commissions of the peace and other institutions of local government. He had to make sure that as far as possible local power structures were respected, but that supporters of the regime were appointed and promoted. If his dealings with Devon and Cornwall were in any way typical, this was work that must have absorbed a great deal of time and effort.[12] Not only did he have to ensure that the right men were picked as sheriffs, he also used the resources of his own household to foster and protect the sons of important families. His correspondence in the course of these dealings is voluminous, and must have kept several secretaries busy. In order to further this local influence, Cromwell also attracted numerous offices, as Keeper of the Jewel House, Clerk of the Hanaper, and Chancellor of the Exchequer, each of which carried a certain amount of patronage, and in April 1534 he became King's Principal Secretary in succession to Stephen Gardiner. This last was an office of the first importance and enabled him to concentrate the very diverse administrative work which already fell to him within a single team of official assistants.[13] It remains an open question whether the initiative for these appointments came from the king or from Cromwell himself, but it is probable that he solicited those positions which he desired when they fell vacant, and that the king obliged him as a mark of the favour and trust which he then enjoyed. One feature of all this acquisition of influence stands out; the number of financial offices which he collected, and this must be seen in terms of his more general scheme for the reorganisation of the royal revenues.[14] The existing system saw the king's income channelled through two main institutions; certain regular revenue, such as the sheriffs' farms went to the Exchequer, while all casual revenue, including the fruits of direct taxation, was paid into the King's Chamber. This was a system which had originated under

King Edward IV, and had been continued by Henry VII. Wolsey, who was not much interested in finance, allowed it to carry on, and it undoubtedly facilitated the king's direct control over expenditure. However, Henry VIII was only interested himself in money when it came to war, and there was not enough of it, so he was not particularly concerned to retain direct control; and that gave Cromwell his opportunity.[15] He had no influence over either the Exchequer or the Treasury of the Chamber, and control was what he desired, so beginning with Augmentations in 1536 he erected a series of revenue courts, secure in the knowledge that he could persuade the king to appoint such officers to run them as he would approve. That these courts were the result of Cromwell's personal initiative is demonstrated by the fact that they did not long survive his fall, being absorbed into a reformed Exchequer in 1554.

The Court of Augmentations may have been in Cromwell's mind for some time, but the need for it was actually created by another statute of the same year, for the dissolving of the smaller monasteries.[16] This was another Act drafted and managed by Cromwell, but with Henry's full knowledge and consent. It used to be argued that the statute was simply motivated by greed, and that the idea came from the secretary as a means of alleviating the immediate financial problem. However it now seems more than likely that it originated with the king, and was motivated at least as much by a desire for religious reform as it was for the assets of the dissolved houses. Henry had never had much time for monks and nuns, following his youthful mentor Erasmus in that respect, and seems to have been genuinely convinced that small monasteries attracted undesirable recruits.[17] It was not that he was opposed to monasticism as such, but that he believed the piety of earlier generations had left the country over-endowed with religious houses, and that many of the inhabitants were not living up to their professions. Cromwell had been appointed Viceregent in Spirituals on 21 January 1535, for the purpose of conducting a royal visitation of the church as a whole, and that was an ongoing operation, but later in that same year he set up special commissions to visit the religious houses. These were authorised by the crown, but the initiative appears to have come from the viceregent, who seems to have considered this the best way to justify a pruning of the establishment.[18] The commissioners were given fairly neutral instructions, and their findings were far from horrendous, but they conveniently confirmed the view that it was the smaller houses which were most deficient. Eventually the Act dissolved all those houses with an income of less that £200 a year, but this was a convenient shorthand for those with fewer than about a dozen inhabitants. Those monks who wished could be transferred to larger houses of the same order, while the others could be given dispensations to return to the world, usually as secular clergy. Nuns were returned to their families, where their welcome was far from assured. The property of the dissolved houses was vested in the crown. This has been described as the first act of 'pure supremacy' in which Henry had indulged, and indeed it would have been unthinkable without his assumption of that status.[19] Wolsey had dissolved a small number of houses earlier, but he had been a papal legate, and had operated in the name of the pope, whereas the king carried out his dissolution using his own authority, and that of the purely secular institution of parliament.

It soon became apparent, however, that this situation was unstable. Thomas Cromwell had been given full powers as viceregent on 18 July 1536, and set about persuading the king that the greater houses would have to go as well. This was not a part of the original plan and the reasons for the change are not altogether clear. However the commissioners were apparently given new instructions, and their reports became markedly less favourable, thus strengthening the viceregent's hand.[20] It may have been the defeat of the protest movement known as the Pilgrimage of Grace, or it may have been the evidence of a strong demand among the gentry and nobility to purchase the lands of those houses which had already been dissolved, but Cromwell decided to start applying pressure to the major houses to undertake 'voluntary' surrenders. Again Henry must have been fully cognisant of this change of policy, and supported it, because no servant would have dared to undertake any such radical action without his full approval. When an abbacy or a priory fell vacant, Cromwell was careful to secure the promotion of men who would cooperate with his programme, and opposition was sporadic and ineffective. Over the three years from 1537 to 1540, the great houses went down one by one, sometimes confessing their shortcomings in fulsome terms.[21] This time there was nowhere for the dispossessed to go, and the distress caused to those with genuine vocations was great. They were pensioned and pitched out into the world without redress. Some tried to maintain a collegiate life in private houses, at least for a time, but most were absorbed into the parochial system, many finding employment as curates and chantry priests. A second statute in 1539 gave their property to the king, in the process recognising surrenders which had already taken place. Unlike the first act it did not decree dissolution.[22] All this property, with a capital value of some £2 million, thus came into the hands of the crown.

It was placed under the control of the Court of Augmentations, and immediately began to be sold off. The last house to surrender was Waltham Abbey in March 1540, and with that surrender a way of life which went back about 1,000 years came to an end. The king's excuse for this drastic action was that monks, friars and nuns were incurably superstitious, but the real reason may well have been that their houses were lingering bastions of papalist sentiment, and that Henry was determined to tolerate no dissent from his position as Supreme Head. After he had carried this programme through to a conclusion, there could no longer be any doubt as to who was in charge of the English Church.

His policy did not go altogether unchallenged. In October 1536 there were rumblings of discontent in Lincolnshire, caused partly at least by the dissolution of the smaller monasteries. There were numerous other grievances behind this rising, and its leadership was not united, but the disappearance of the minor religious houses, which, it was argued, had provided employment and poor relief to the distressed, was one cause behind which they could all unite. Other causes were rumours that the king intended to seize the property of parish churches, and demand exorbitant taxes; general discontent with the direction of royal policy, which seemed to favour heretics like Archbishop Cranmer; and the dishonourable treatment accorded to the Princess Mary.[23] There was also some gentry discontent with the position being assumed in the county by the Duke of Suffolk, following his marriage to the Lincolnshire heiress, Catherine Willoughby. This caused some gentlemen to join the rising, and the king treated their subsequent justification of having been coerced by the commons with justifiable scepticism. For a short while the movement assumed formidable dimensions, and several thousand men assembled at Lincoln in mid-October. However, the dependence of the committed rebels on gentry leadership proved their undoing, because having made their protest, most of the gentlemen were only too happy to settle for a royal pardon and go home.[24] Meanwhile, the revolt had spread across the Humber into Yorkshire, where it flared up sporadically across much of the county. Here, as in Lincolnshire, the motivation varied, but might broadly be described as conservative and religious. The leadership, however, was different. Gentlemen like Sir Thomas Percy, a brother of the sixth Earl of Northumberland, endeavoured with some success to raise the traditional feudal loyalty to his family, giving the rising a very old fashioned appearance.[25] More particularly Robert Aske, a lawyer and a Percy dependant, rapidly emerged as the real ideological commander, formulating the rebels demands very much in terms of the dissolved religious houses. These, and other aristocratic leaders such as Lord Darcy and Sir Robert Constable, gave some coherence to a movement which was otherwise local and spontaneous in its inspiration. They may have had as many as 30,000 men under their command when they advanced to Doncaster early in December. The king fumed and raged, but he had no forces available to resist such a force, and he authorised the Duke of Norfolk on his behalf to make concessions, including a pardon if they agreed to disperse.[26] By the time that this negotiation took place, it had become obvious that two elements were working in the king's favour. In the first place the Earls of Shrewsbury and Derby held aloof, not because they supported royal policy but because their loyalty to the crown was in question, and in the second place the Pilgrims saw themselves as protesters, not rebels. Their aim was to persuade the king to change his mind, not to overthrow him, and Henry's concessions seemed to promise just that. When he received the king's response, Aske worked extremely hard to persuade his followers to accept the offer made. There were those, particularly among the original commons' leaders, who disagreed and were all in favour of pressing on to the south, but Aske succeeded in overruling them, and the conciliatory offer was accepted.[27]

The so-called 'Pontefract articles', to which this offer was addressed, started by rejecting the heresies of Luther, Hus and Wycliffe, and then asked the king to reconsider his ecclesiastical supremacy by returning it to Rome. There then followed clauses relating to the legitimacy of the Princess Mary, and the restoration of dissolved monasteries and friaries. Cromwell, Cranmer and other heretics were to receive 'condign punishment' and (rather incongruously) the statute of handguns and crossbows was to be repealed.[28] Henry, of course, had no intention of reconsidering any of these aspects of his policy, but he made it appear that he might, and that gave Aske sufficient grounds to accept the offer, and disperse his followers. Other considerations also affected this decision. Many of his gentlemen allies were uneasy at their exposed position, and shared his fundamental loyalty; also the rank and file were unsettled at being so far from their bases, and unwilling to face a clash with royal troops which would have resulted from pursuing their aims further. So they went home, protected by a royal pardon and Aske went to court for the Christmas to pursue further negotiations.[29] Mary had carefully avoided giving any countenance to the Pilgrims, and the king had no intention of abandoning Cromwell and Cranmer to their tender mercies. To what extent he might have honoured his promises if the Bigod rebellion in January 1537 had not supervened, we do not know. As it was, that rising (which had nothing to do with the original Pilgrimage) gave him the perfect excuse to abandon all the concessions which he had made, including his pardon. About 170 of the original Pilgrims, including the leaders, Aske and Darcy, were executed, the promised parliament at York was abandoned, and the king's policies continued as before.[30] In other circumstances, or with other leaders, the Pilgrimage of Grace could have been a serious threat to the stability of England. If the emperor had heeded the urgings of his ambassador Eustace Chapuys and intervened, or if Reginald Pole's mission in support had worked, Henry could well have been overthrown. Pole had been created cardinal and sent north as soon as news of the insurrection reached Rome, but by the time that he arrived in the Low Countries it was all over bar the punishments, and he was left with nothing to work on.

Cromwell kept a low profile while the Pilgrimage was ongoing, but showed no signs of relaxing his efforts on the king's behalf. He had been created Lord Privy Seal on 29 June 1536, and moved the focus of his power into that office with immediate effect. This promotion occurred in the midst of his efforts to protect Mary from the consequences of her own obstinacy, and may have been partly a reward for his services in getting rid of Anne Boleyn.[31] For that purpose he had formed an uneasy alliance with the conservatives in the council, and no doubt that facilitated the dismissal of the Earl of Wiltshire as Lord Privy Seal. The earl (Thomas Boleyn) was Anne's father, and although not otherwise penalised for her misdemeanours, lost his preferment and was excluded from the court. Had the Pilgrimage not been halted at Doncaster, Cromwell's security arrangements in the rest of the country might have been put to a severe test, but it did not happen and his networks continued in place. There was plenty of discontent, but it did not come to a head. Hostile things were being said, not only about Cromwell but also about the king; he was 'a mole who should be put down' and 'a tyrant worse than Nero'. However we only know about these mutterings because they were reported to the Lord Privy Seal, and the conclusion must be that his informers were still in full working order.[32] In dealing with the Pilgrims, Henry chose to trust the Dukes of Norfolk and Suffolk, both of them religious conservatives and opposed to Cromwell, but they did not in any sense take over his confidential relationship. Norfolk was the king's senior councillor and Lord Treasurer of England, but his alliance with the leading religious conservative, Stephen Gardiner, Bishop of Winchester, was uneasy and for the time being neither of them influenced royal policy. In spite of the birth of Prince Edward in October 1537, Henry was still extremely anxious about the succession, and positively paranoid about the activities of Cardinal Pole, any contact with whom could be construed as treason. It was this fear which gave Cromwell the basis for his second coup in the summer of 1538, when on the basis of a tip-off, Geoffrey Pole, the cardinal's brother, was arrested on a charge of corresponding with the exiled prelate.[33] Under extreme pressure, which may have included the threat of torture, Geoffrey implicated his brother, Lord Montague, his mother, Countess of Salisbury, and Henry Courtenay, Marquis of Exeter. Significantly these were all people with a claim to the throne should Henry or Edward 'miscarry', and that was deemed to be the objective of their letters to Reginald. They were also known to be out of sympathy with the king's radical religious policies, and were suspect to Cromwell for that reason.[34] The Marchioness of Exeter and the Countess of Salisbury had been close to Catherine of Aragon, and had earlier been implicated in the affair of the Nun of Kent, Elizabeth Barton, who had uttered prophecies threatening the king, and had been executed for treason in 1533. In Cornwall, which was a centre of conservative religious sentiment, it was alleged that Courtenay was the true heir to the throne, and that the time was coming when he would wear the garland and 'bring better days'. Such sentiments were undoubtedly treasonable, but they should not have affected the main parties.[35] Courtenay and Montague were nevertheless indicted, along with Sir Edward Neville, found guilty and executed on 9 December 1538. They had indeed protected and helped others whose agenda was more explicitly treasonable than their own, and they had corresponded in a friendly fashion with the cardinal, whose objective was explicitly Henry's overthrow. However, the case against them was purely circumstantial, and they died mainly for who they were rather than for anything which they had done. Shortly after, as though to emphasise the problem, Reginald turned up again in northern Europe, with the same agenda as before, this time trying to take advantage of the Treaty of Toledo to motivate Charles V and Francis I to join forces against the schismatic King of England. This was no more successful than the earlier mission, but it provided Henry with an excuse (if he needed one) to proceed further against Margaret Pole.[36] She was placed under house arrest at Cowdray Park in Sussex and fiercely interrogated. She confessed nothing beyond her affection for her sons, and was not tried. Instead she was attainted by Act of Parliament and was taken to the Tower in June 1539. There she remained until a minor conspiracy in Yorkshire in 1541, which involved a number of members of the Neville family and was linked to the Pilgrimage of Grace, brought about her execution.[37] She was sixty-eight years old, had lived through four reigns and had seen her father, brother, and son executed – such was the peril of proximity to the throne. Meanwhile Geoffrey had been pardoned as a reward for his compliance, and half-mad with remorse, had taken himself off to the Continent in search of Reginald and forgiveness for what he had done.

The fate of the Poles and the Courtenays demonstrates not only the fragility of the king's reflexes on the subject of the succession, but also of the battle which was ongoing in the council and at court between those who supported Cromwell's evangelical agenda and those who wished to preserve the continuities of the Catholic faith. Henry's own position seems to have varied, now supporting the translation of the Bible, which was an evangelical priority, and now condemning John Lambert as a sacramentary. In reality, however, the king's doctrine was consistent, although idiosyncratic.[38] He believed that the bible should be available to all those who could profit by reading it, but that as the sacred text it should be treated with proper respect. So in 1538 he approved of Cromwell's articles requiring the Bible to be placed in every church, and then in April 1539 restricted the reading of it to clergy and gentry, on the grounds that it was being 'railed at and disputed' in taverns and alehouses.[39] Similarly he never wavered in his devotion to the mass, and woe betide anyone who denied transubstantiation in his hearing. The condemnation of Lambert was supported by Cromwell and Cranmer because he denied the 'real presence', which the Lord Privy Seal and the archbishop (at that time) both upheld. *The Bishops' Book* of 1537, which appeared to countenance the idea of justification by faith alone, never received the royal seal of approval. Doctrinally Henry remained a Catholic, and Lutheran and Zwinglian ideas were outlawed.

There was no reason in canon law why the scriptures should not be translated into the vernacular, and Archbishop Arundel's constitutions merely forbade unauthorised translations. There was no reason why the Coverdale Bible or the Great Bible should not be used, because these had been properly authorised – by the Supreme Head.[40] The Act of Six Articles, upholding the traditional doctrine and use of the mass, came as a shock to the evangelicals, but it should not have done because it did not say anything that Henry had not been saying for years; and John Foxe's assertion that it came about as a result of the malign influence of the Bishop of Winchester is an explanation too far. In terms of the church, Henry was radical, denying the papal authority and dissolving the monasteries, but in terms of belief he was relentlessly orthodox. Foxe was puzzled by Henry's seeming inconsistencies, and ended by attributing them to the influence of rival groups of councillors, but in truth the king remained very much in charge, and the apparent inconsistencies were within his own head.[41]

Part of the problem arose, both at the time and since, from reading the Lord Privy Seal's lips rather than the king's on the assumption that they must be identical. In fact that was not the case, and Cromwell stretched his favour on a number of occasions. For instance he attempted to rescue William Tyndale in 1535, and continued to use Robert Barnes in a semi-official capacity in spite of his suspect sermons. Throughout his period in power he continued to patronise and protect Evangelical preachers, and even when they strayed over the boundary into heresy he used his authority as viceregent to get them off or reduce their penances.[42] Henry tolerated this, because he recognised Cromwell's zeal for the supremacy, and that was what mattered to him most. However the Six Articles were clearly enacted against his advice and without his participation, and thus represented a victory for Gardiner, Wriothesley and the Howards. It was no accident that the measure was introduced into the House of Lords by the duke, although it clearly represented the king's wishes. Henry thoughtfully gave Cranmer leave to be absent from the parliament while the Bill was in passage, because he knew that it offended his conscience,[43] but no such indulgence was extended to Cromwell. Perhaps he did not take the Lord Privy Seal's conscience very seriously, or perhaps he wished to make it clear that Cromwell did not enjoy any monopoly of the king's confidence. He was quite capable of listening to other counsel, and of making up his own mind when the issues were controversial. If so, it was a warning which his servant was slow to heed; he seems to have accepted it as simply another statute which needed to be enforced, albeit not one which he would implement with any enthusiasm.

Meanwhile, Catherine was growing up at Horsham and Lambeth, and indulging in her sexual adventures. Her father died in March 1539, leaving his children nothing but debts and a modest estate which was divided between the boys, George, Henry and Charles, all of whom were of age. If Catherine received anything from her impecunious sire we have no record of it, and there was certainly no marriage portion. Unless Francis Dereham chose to marry her, she was going to be very much on her own. At what point her uncle, the duke, began to spy potential in her we do not know, but he seems to have assumed responsibility for her after her father's death. The court was the place for a young lady to make her way in the world, and he managed to secure a place for her in the household which was being assembled for the new queen, Anne of Cleves, in

November 1539.[44] More than that, he got her into the queen's Privy Chamber. There seems to have been no particular plan in this; she was just another Howard in a position to be useful to the family. It was only when Henry's fourth marriage was clearly in difficulties, in March and April 1540, that he began to perceive a more promising outcome, and assiduously encouraged the interest which the king was beginning to show in his kinswoman. By the summer of 1540, the plot was ripe.

4
The Summer of 1540

Anne enjoyed about six months as queen consort. She had been married on 6 January, a ceremony which had been preceded by the signing of a solemn document on behalf of William of Cleves, acknowledging Henry to be an orthodox Catholic who had been treated unjustly by the papacy. The purpose of this declaration being apparently to discourage any speculation, either at home or in Germany that the marriage would lead to further religious reform in England.[1] The king's intentions in this respect at any rate were clear, which was more than could be said for the wedding itself. Before the ceremony, and in the privacy of his own closet, Henry had confided to Cromwell that 'if it were not to satisfy the world and my realm, I would not do that I must do this day for none earthly thing', which was not the most promising of starts.[2] Anne had been escorted to her nuptials by two German nobles who were to give her away on behalf of the duke, and when Henry entered the gallery where the wedding was to take place, she curtsied to him solemnly. They had then taken up their position, he on the right hand and she on the left. Cranmer had officiated, and started by asking each of them whether they knew any just impediment to the matrimony to be concluded between them. The king, who must have had serious doubts in that direction on account of the Lorraine pre-contract, replied that he did not. They had then exchanged their vows, and been duly proclaimed man and wife. After suitable prayers and blessing from the archbishop, they had proceeded hand in hand into his closet to hear the Mass of the Trinity, a gesture of orthodoxy upon which Henry had insisted. They had then changed their apparel, and proceeded to the traditional wedding feast, which must have occupied the middle of the day, because the queen had thereafter attended Evensong. Following the service, Henry and Anne had then supped together in public, before enjoying the masks and dances which had ended the evening.[3] Considering that Anne was a foreign princess, the festivities had been remarkably restrained. Usually such celebrations would continue for several days, but in this case nothing else seems to have happened until the jousts which took place almost a week later. This had not been due to any disappointment with Anne, but like the decision to marry at Greenwich rather than Westminster, had been partly dictated by considerations of economy, and partly by the fact that the king had chosen to be married on a feast day in the season of Epiphany. Apart from the wedding feast itself, all the festivities were those appropriate to the season.

Ribald curiosity accompanied the wedding night. After the bed had been solemnly blessed, the couple were allowed to retire in private, but the eavesdroppers (of whom there were several) attended at the chamber door.[4] They might not have heard anything very interesting, because according to the later testimony of Dr William Butts, Henry decided not to attempt consummation on the first night, which means that Anne's apparently innocent question the following morning may have been ironical. However Henry admitted that his 'nature hath abhorred her', and it seems that earnest attempts at intercourse on the third and fourth nights were unsuccessful.[5] It may be that he was attempting to follow an old tradition in delaying consummation to the third night in the hope of begetting a healthy male child, and to demonstrate that he had not entered into the union though 'carnal concupiscence'. The begetting of children was a sacred duty, not to be entered into lightly, and the belief was that God would intervene to make a pious couple fruitful. However, dislike of Anne's person seems to have been the controlling factor in this situation. He continued to sleep with her at least until Shrovetide, which fell on 10 February, but later confessed that he left her as good a maid as he found her. After observing a ritual abstinence during Lent, he seems to have resumed his efforts after Easter (28 March), but with no better success than before. At first only Cromwell seems to have been aware of these difficulties, but he confided in Anne's chamberlain, the Earl of Rutland and by Whitsun, which was 16 May, his personal attendants generally were aware of the problem.[6] Cromwell urged Rutland to encourage the queen to be more agreeable towards her husband. The woman was generally held to be responsible for these matrimonial malfunctions, but it is by no means clear that Rutland transmitted this well-meant advice to the queen. As Retha Warnicke has observed, 'early modern Christians did not recognize the psychological dimension of impotency as it is understood today...' but rather looked for external causes; the anger of God or sorcery being the commonest explanations.[7] Henry seems genuinely to have believed that (as with Anne Boleyn) he was the victim of witchcraft. Either that, or he had failed to keep God's rules with respect to marriage, although that can hardly have been the case as far as Anne was concerned. It would be nearer the mark to say that his lack of 'goodwill' towards his bride was the root cause of his malfunction. Anne is not known to have responded either to criticism or advice, and was not suspected of being a witch. The identity of that malign individual is not known.

While the king struggled in private with his sexual incapacity, they appeared in public as a contented couple. Before he departed for Cleves on 19 January, Henry Olisleger commented specifically on their harmonious relationship. Henry presented her with jewellery in lavish quantities, and before they departed the German nobles who had accompanied her also received generous gifts of plate and money, which were interpreted as a sign of royal satisfaction.[8] Anne presided gracefully at the jousts which were held on 11 January and distributed the prizes, although it is reasonably certain that she had never been called upon to perform such an office in the past. The religious reformers misinterpreted the significance of the marriage. A certain John Butler rote to Henry Bullinger on 24 February that the state of the gospel in England would now be much more secure, because Anne was a pious woman by whom the faith would be promoted. This did not happen, of course, because during her time as queen she did not intervene at all in the life of the church, and assiduously attended all the traditional rites and observances. Her attitude towards the English bible, for which she would have had no use, remains unknown. Nor did she confide her sexual problems to any of her German attendants. When most of them withdrew on 19 January, she sent word to her mother and her brother, thanking them for arranging her marriage to Henry; 'none other,' she alleged, 'would content her mind so well'.[9] However it was her body rather than her mind which was in question. They even managed to have a routine disagreement over the presence in the court of the Lady Mary, the king's daughter, because Anne objected to her living on the 'queen's side', and became quite stubborn over the matter, possibly because she had not been consulted in the first place. Chapuys noted that Mary did not treat the queen with the same respect that she had shown to her predecessor, and that may have been the root cause of the trouble.[10]

On 4 February the king and queen, accompanied by many noblemen, had travelled from Greenwich to Westmister by river. A display, similar to that which had greeted her at Blackheath, was deployed on the Thames, and the Lord Mayor and aldermen appeared in their traditional barges, complete with minstrels, who played vigorously in order to be heard above the noise of the salvos fired from the Tower of London and from royal warships anchored in the river. There were no pageants, but the king was displayed to his loving subjects as a contented husband, and this was something of a triumph for Anne of Cleves.[11] A few days later the Duke of Norfolk was sent on mission to France, because whatever his inclinations, Henry could not afford to abandon Anne until he was assured of the friendship of Francis, and that the latter's recent rapprochement with Charles V had given him every cause to doubt. On 23 February Norfolk was able to report the success of his mission. Francis, he declared, was Henry's friend and was not preparing to go to war against him. At the same time, he was anxious to preserve his treaty with the emperor, and concerned about the delays in settling the future of Milan. Finally, it would be desirable to withdraw Edmund

Bonner as resident ambassador in France, because his tactless behaviour had made many enemies. This last point had already been taken, and Sir John Wallop had been appointed to replace him.[12] When the duke reached England on 1 March, there was a marked relaxation of tension on all sides. The king could now afford to drop the Cleves alliance because he was assured of the friendship of France.

Anne's last appearance in public as queen was during the festivities which marked May Day, the official beginning of summer. Throughout March and April preparations for the jousts which marked that season had been under-way, and Marrillac, the French ambassador, had speculated that these would also be used to celebrate Anne's coronation. The queen wanted to be crowned, but did not want to raise the matter with her husband, so she instructed Carl Harst, who was her personal adviser, to broach the subject indirectly with Cromwell. He did so, but without any success.[13] Had Anne been pregnant the story might have been very different, but Henry had no intention of honouring an unconsummated union in such a fashion. Behind the scenes, he was already moving to dissolve his marriage, and had his eye on Catherine Howard as her successor. Nevertheless the king and queen presided together at the May Day jousts, which lasted from 30 April to 7 May, and supped and dined in public at the open house in Durham Place, which accompanied the tournament. By 20 June even Harst had noticed that all was not well, because on that day Anne complained to him about the attentions that the king was paying to Catherine.[14] He tried to reassure her that this was just a casual flirtation, but she was not to be comforted, and with reason, because on 24 June the council instructed that she remove herself to Richmond, allegedly because of plague in the city. Anne enjoyed the pomp and ceremony of the court, and was deeply depressed by this rustication. On the following day she was visited by commissioners from Henry to explain to her (through an interpreter) that her marriage was invalid. Henry had been working in that direction since at least March. The pre-contract with the Duke of Lorraine was a non-starter, because it had been fully repudiated by all parties, a fact made clear by documents which he had received from Cleves in answer to a specific request.[15] The king was therefore driven back on non-consummation as the ground for an annulment, and had clearly made up his mind to that effect by the middle of June. On 6 July, at the carefully choreographed request of the parliament, the case was committed to 'the clergy of England', a select group which would once have been Cromwell's Viceregal synod. However Cromwell had fallen by then, and it was presided over by Archbishop Cranmer. By 9 July it was all over and the ecclesiastical 'court' had pronounced that the Cleves marriage did not exist and never had done.[16] Considering the distressed state that she was in at the end of June, Anne accepted her dismissal with remarkable stoicism, signing her letter of submission to the king 'Anna, daughter of Cleves'. She may even have been relieved that she would no longer be compelled to endure his attempts to have intercourse. She was content to accept whatever the king might decree. Henry, perhaps out of relief at her submissiveness, was generous; granting her lands to the value of £3,000 a year and several royal houses, so long as she remained in England.[17] Rather surprisingly she showed no desire to return to Cleves, and the duke her brother was forced to accept her decision with as good a grace as he could muster. After all, if she was not disposed to make a fuss, why should he?

After 24 June they never met again as husband and wife; when they encountered in August, Henry was remarried and Anne was his 'good sister'.

The politics of this annulment were intimately bound up with the fall of Thomas Cromwell, which occurred at the same time. He was arrested at a council meeting on 10 June and committed to the Tower. However it would not be true to say that he fell simply because he had persuaded the king into a failed marriage, because he was perfectly capable of securing an annulment once he was convinced that that was what Henry wanted. He fell for a variety of reasons, and the story is complicated by French rumours that he was plotting to marry the Princess Mary, and thus in due course become king – rumours which were without the smallest foundation.[18] Nor was he the leader of an 'evangelical faction' within the Council, unless the unwavering support of Archbishop Cranmer constitutes a party. He fell because his enemies in the council, of whom Stephen Gardiner was the most prominent, succeeded in convincing the king that he had abused his position as Viceregent in Spirituals, and, in that he occasionally acted on his own initiative, informing the king after the event, such charges were justified. However, Cromwell was not a Protestant, let alone a sacramentary (that is one who denies the real presence in the Eucharistic elements). In 1536 he had signed the Ten Articles, which were the most radical formula to be issued during the reign. Nevertheless these articles did not deviate from the Catholic position on the Eucharistic elements, or on the need for good works to contribute towards a person's salvation, and their resemblance to the Augsburg Confession was largely superficial. Moreover their title reflects the fact that Henry was fully involved; 'Articles Devised by the

King's Majesty to stabilise Christian quietness and unity among us, and to avoid contentious opinions.'[19] In August 1536 he did issue injunctions to enforce the Articles that were rather more hostile to images, relics and other popular practices than were the Articles themselves, but there is no reason to suppose that he did this without Henry's knowledge and consent. Indeed the injunctions themselves were later known as the king's. Any resemblance to the Augsburg Confession can be explained by the fact that Cromwell was angling for an alliance with the Schmalkaldic League at that point, and indeed foreign policy considerations loom large in his actions as viceregent, actions which were always scrupulously agreed with the king beforehand. His further abortive negotiations with the League in the summer of 1539, and the eventual conclusion of a treaty with Cleves, have to be seen in the same light.[20] Cromwell may well have been embarrassed in this connection by the passage of the Act of Six Articles, but there is no evidence that he opposed its passage, as there is in the case of Cranmer. Indeed one report from the court in August 1539 described the viceregent as 'utterly persuaded' by the Act, and it was he who induced Cranmer to accept the clause on clerical celibacy, although that necessitated the withdrawal of Margaret and the children to the Continent. After the passage of the Act, and knowing his archbishop's mind, Henry took the extraordinary step of sending Cromwell and other councillors to Lambeth to dine with Cranmer as an indication of his continued favour.[21]

Where Cromwell did take risks was in his protection of heretical preachers – or those accused of being such – who frequently appealed to him against their condemnation by ecclesiastical courts. He reduced their penances, persuaded them to preach recantation sermons, and sometimes got them off altogether. It would probably be true to say that Henry was indulgent towards these activities, until he chose not to be in the summer of 1540. He also used suspect agents in his negotiations, particularly with the German protestants, and Robert Barnes's numerous trips to Germany in an official capacity have to be seen in this light.[22] Barnes was constantly in trouble for his evangelical sermons, but here again the king was fully cognisant, and approved his use in this connection because of the need to send an envoy who would be congenial to the Leaguers. More immediately relevant to Cromwell's downfall were the circumstances in Calais in the spring of 1540. There the Lord Deputy, Lord Lisle was accused of treasonable correspondence with Reginald Pole, and it emerged in the course of the investigation that one Adam Damplip, who was one of the witnesses, was a sacramentary who had been protected by Cromwell (and Cranmer) until he was arrested, imprisoned and eventually burned for heresy.[23] That protection was required by the need to build a case against Lisle, but it is fairly certain that the king did not know of it, or at least did not know of Damplip's views on the Eucharist when he approved of it. This was the last straw as far as Henry was concerned, and his viceregent quite suddenly became a heretic, and a promoter of heretics. That this apparently dramatic conversion was due to the influence of his enemies is a natural assumption, but hard to prove. The Duke of Norfolk was his sworn enemy, and was a powerful man with backers in the council, but he was not a diligent attender at meetings, and spent much of his time in the crown's service elsewhere. He was also conservative in his religious preferences, but lacked the political astuteness to have exploited an opening of this kind. Stephen Gardiner, Bishop of

Winchester, is the likeliest candidate; he also had his backers, was opposed to Cromwell on most issues, and was regularly present at the council board. He could well have exploited his regular access to the king to influence his mind, but no contemporary document actually says so. When parliament reassembled on 12 April, the Lord Privy Seal appeared very much in charge. It was he who spoke in deadly earnest on the subject of religious unity, and he undoubtedly expressed the king's mind.

> One side call the other papists and the other again calls them heretics, both naughty and not to be borne; and that the less so because they miserably abuse the Holy word of God and the Scriptures...[24]

The king favoured neither side, 'but as becometh a Christian Prince, professes the true Christian faith'. Two committees were established to round off the Act of Six Articles with authoritative statements of doctrine and ceremonial, and their composition shows that the evangelical party was losing ground. Nevertheless Cromwell remained very much in charge of the parliamentary agenda, which included the confiscation of the property of the Knights of St John, and on 18 April the king elevated him to the Earldom of Essex and made him Lord Great Chamberlain.[25] The king's mind seems to have been very much in the balance at that point, because it is inconceivable that such a gesture would have been made to lure Cromwell into a sense of false security. Nevertheless he was under pressure and shortly after parliament reassembled on 30 May he ordered the arrest of Bishop Sampson of Chichester and Dr Nicholas Wotton, two religious conservatives. Sampson has been identified as

Gardiner's right-hand man, and both were arrested on the pretext of papalist conspiracy. These arrests seem to have been carried out on Cromwell's own authority, but the king was wholly supportive and it was rumoured that the Lord Privy Seal had his eye on five other bishops, who may well have included Gardiner himself.[26] Rumours flew thick and fast; Barnes was to be released and Latimer reinstated. However these reports seem to have originated from within the evangelical camp, and in retrospect look very much like whistling in the dark. For a few days more, Cromwell appeared to be completely successful where it really mattered, with the king. According to Ralf Sadler, who wrote in the first week of June, Henry was not at all impressed with Sampson's defence of his actions, and prepared to consider Latimer's case sympathetically, after further discussion with the Lord Privy Seal.[27] However, appearances were deceptive. Cromwell had been very little at court during the previous month, being busy in parliament, and in that time his enemies had gained the king's ear, Gardiner, who was presumably fighting for his career if not his life, being particularly successful. At some point between 5 and 10 June, Henry turned around, and Cromwell was arrested at a council meeting on the latter day. He was hoist with his own petard, because it had been in a very similar fashion that he had 'bounced' the king into condemning Anne Boleyn in 1536. Henry was prone to these sudden decisions, and how long he had been contemplating such a move is unknown. The affair in Calais seems to have convinced him that he was surrounded by enemies, and it is clear from Cromwell's address to the House of Lords that he saw papists and heretics as equally undesirable. Papists were clearly traitors, but he remained to be persuaded that heretics were just as bad, and that was the measure of

Gardiner's success in May 1540. Quite suddenly the Cleves alliance, and the detested marriage that went with it, fell into place alongside Cromwell's extensive use of his powers as viceregent, his patronage of dubious preachers, and his friendships with heretics, which added up to a monstrous conspiracy to hijack the royal supremacy for Evangelical purposes.[28] Because they were his best allies against the papists, he was in danger of finding himself committed to the reformers, and he intended to retain his freedom of action, so he turned upon his Lord Privy Seal as the architect and manager of this subversive programme.

Cromwell was stripped of his garter and other insignia of honour by the Duke of Norfolk at the time of his arrest, and a few days later wrote to the king from the Tower, protesting his innocence of the crimes charged against him, but submitting entirely to Henry's will. His goods and houses had been seized on 10 June, and that was an ominous sign, but he wrote not in self-justification but primarily to plead for mercy.[29] He knew his master well enough to know that argument would be useless in his case, and his only hope lay in complete self-abasement. He did, however, protest with justice that he was not a sacramentary, realising the king's abhorrence of that radical position, and the role that such a charge had probably played in bringing about his downfall. He was never tried, it probably being decided that many of the charges against him touched the king's honour, but rather proceeded against by Act of Attainder, a method that he had developed himself to deal with troublesome people against whom no adequate case in law could be framed. As set out in the Bill, the charges mostly related to the abuse of his power. Firstly, that he had taken upon himself to release those convicted of misprision of treason, and had not proceeded against suspects.

Secondly, that he had sold, 'contrary to proclamation', licences to export a variety of commodities, without due authority to do so. Thirdly, that he had issued commissions in many 'great and weighty causes', without the king's knowledge.[30] He had also granted passports to aliens and others 'to pass without search', again on his own authority. The sixth and eighth clauses of the Bill accused him of issuing heretical writings and translations, of setting heretics at liberty and of refusing to listen to charges of heresy brought to his attention. He had also licensed heretics to preach; all abuses of his position as Viceregent in Spirituals. It could be argued that he had indeed done these things, but that in every case he was covered, either by the general powers conferred upon him or by the king's specific permission. However Henry's memory was short in such matters, and the general powers had not been designed to counter charges of this kind, being very vague in their nature. Other clauses charged him that, 'being a person of poor and low degree' he had despised the nobility, and that having obtained 'by oppression, bribery [and] extort power' great wealth, he had resorted to threats against them; particularly that in the parish of St Martins in the Fields on 31 January 1540, when he had declared that 'if the lord would handle him so he would give them such a breakfast as never was made in England'.[31] Of all the charges against him this is the most plausible, but it amounts to *scandalum magnatum*, not high treason. The treason (insofar as it existed) resided in the tenth clause of the bill; 'supposing himself to be fully able by force and strength' to defend his position, he had declared on 31 March 1539 in the City of London, that the teaching of Barnes and others accused of heresy was good. More to the point, 'if the king would turn from it, yet I would not turn; and if the king did turn and

1. Catherine Howard as queen, from the stained glass window representing her as the Queen of Sheba, and Henry VIII as King Solomon. King's College Chapel, Cambridge.

2. Henry VIII, with Henry VII in the background; from the cartoon by Hans Holbein in the National Portrait Gallery.
Opposite: 3. Catherine of Aragon, Henry's first queen. Henry had a prolonged struggle to dissolve their marriage.

KATHERINA VXOR HENRICI . . VIII.

ANNA BOLLINA ꞏ VXOR HE[NRICI]

Opposite: 4. Anne Boleyn, Henry's second queen, whom he had executed for adultery in 1536.
Above: 5. The tomb of Henry Fitzroy, Duke of Richmond, Henry's illegitimate son, in St Michael's church, Framlingham, Suffolk.
Right: 6. Elizabeth ('Bessie') Blount, the mother of the Duke of Richmond, from her funeral effigy.

7. Jane Seymour, Henry's third queen and the mother of his heir; by Hans Holbein the Younger.

Left: 8. Henry's sixth and last queen, Catherine Parr, from a stained glass window at Sudeley Castle. After Henry's death Catherine married Thomas, Lord Seymour of Sudeley, and is buried in the church there. *Above*: 9. Henry's fourth wife, Anne of Cleves. The king had this marriage annulled after five months on the grounds of non-consummation.

10. Stephen Gardiner, Bishop of Winchester. A leader of the conservative party on the council in the 1540s, Henry deliberately excluded him from his panel of executors.

Above left: 11. Thomas Wolsey, Cardinal Archbishop of York and Lord Chancellor. From a drawing by Jacques Lebouque.
Above right: 12. Funeral effigy of Thomas Boleyn, Earl of Wiltshire. Thomas was deprived of his office as Lord Privy Seal following his daughter's execution in May 1536, but was not otherwise penalised.

13. The tomb of Thomas Howard, 3rd Duke of Norfolk and Catherine's uncle, He died in 1554 and was originally interred in the church of the dissolved abbey at Thetford in Norfolk. He was later moved to Framlingham in Suffolk, where this monument was erected.

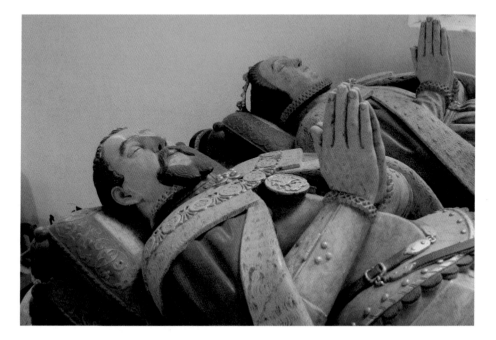

Above: 14. Henry Howard, Earl of Surrey, the son of the 3rd Duke of Norfolk and cousin of Catherine. He was a wild young man, and was executed for treason in January 1547, just a few days before Henry's death.

Opposite: 15. The title page of Henry's Great Bible (1539), which shows him handing the Word of God to the spirituality, headed by Thomas Cranmer, the Archbishop of Canterbury, and to the laity, headed by Thomas Cromwell, the Lord Privy Seal.

¶ The Byble in Englyshe, that is to saye the content of all the holy scrypture, bothe of ye olde and newe testament truly translated after the veryte of the Hebrue and Greke textes, by ye dylygent studye of dyuerse excellent learned men, expert in the forsayde tonges.

¶ Prynted by Rychard Grafton & Edward Whitchurch.

Cum priuilegio ad imprimendum solum.
1539.

King Henry the eyght.

Labels within the plan:

Scotland Yard

Great Hall,
by Wolsey, 1528

The court

F

The court

Tennis court
G

Preaching
place ▸

'Holbein' gate

H

Privy bridge

King St Gate

F

Court

Kings street

Chanon row

B

Wesmynster Hall (the seat of the law courts)

A

E

Abby

E

E

E

Starre Chamber

House of Commons
(formerly chapel of St Stephen's)
from 1547 until the fire of 1834

House of Lords

Court of Requests

The Queens bridge

Henry VII's chapel

Opposite: 16. Henry VIII in a formal session of the council. Henry did not attend regular meetings of the council, so this would have been a special session, when he had some momentous news to impart.
Above: 17. A plan of the palaces of Westminster and Whitehall, from a later version of the map known by the name of Ralph Agas, although not by him. The Thames was the main highway connecting Westminster with Hampton Court and Greenwich.

19. Henry VIII's new palace of Nonsuch, built in approximate imitation of Francis I's palace of Chambord. It was unfinished at Henry's death, and was demolished in the late seventeenth century

Opposite: 18. Ladies' fashions at the court of Henry VIII, from a sketch by Hans Holbein.
Above: 20. Hampton Court. Wolsey's palace which he gave to Henry VIII in 1525. The King carried out extensive building work there.

Above: 21. Greenwich palace, where Henry VIII was born. It remained one of his favourite residences, but nothing of the Tudor building now survives above ground.
Left: 22. Thomas Cranmer, Archbishop of Canterbury, by Gerhard Flicke.

23. Henry VIII at the Field of Cloth of Gold, his 'summit' meeting with Francis I of France in 1520.

Above: 24. The meeting of the Kings at the Field of Cloth of Gold, with Henry VIII on the left and Francis I on the right. Taken from a plaster cast of a bas-relief in the Hotel de Bourgtheroulde, a noble town house in Rouen.
Right: 25. A late version of Henry VIII's Great Seal, reflecting the Royal Supremacy over the Church.

26. The Tower of London, taken from a painting by Claes Visscher, 1616.

27. The Chapel of St Peter ad Vincula and the site of the scaffold on Tower Green, where Catherine was beheaded by a single axe blow on Monday 13 February 1542. She was later buried in the Chapel.

all the people, I would fight in the field in my own person, with my sword in my hand, against him and all other'. This he had reiterated 'with oaths and affirmations'. If this was true, then it was treason by words under the Act of 1534, but it sounds most uncharacteristic of the cautious Cromwell known to history, and the prospect of the Viceregent in Spirituals fighting against the king in some kind of religious rebellion does not make any kind of sense. His whole dilemma derived from the fact that his position had depended entirely upon the king, and when Henry decided to destroy him, he had no other resource to resort to. Because the king was so obviously behind it, the Bill of Attainder encountered no opposition in either house, and was presented for the royal assent on 30 June.[32] Then the king appears to have hesitated. On that same day Cromwell addressed another letter to him; 'I am a most woeful prisoner, ready to take the death when it shall please God and your Majesty, and yet the frail flesh inciteth me to call to your grace for mercy and pardon...'[33] This may have moved Henry, but if so Gardiner and Norfolk were on hand to stiffen his resolution, and his hesitation seems to have been caused as much by the demands of his annulment as by sympathy with his prisoner. He might have needed Cromwell's testimony in that tangled affair, and when it became clear that he did not, he gave his assent to the attainder. It may be noticed that neither his role in the Cleves negotiation nor his sacramentarianism featured in the Act; the first because even Henry could not deny that it had been carried out with his full knowledge and consent, and the latter because it would have brought the case within the jurisdiction of the spiritual courts – a complication which the king had no intention of suffering. So Thomas Cromwell went to his death on Tower Green on 28 July 1540, and the Earldom of Essex was extinguished by his attainder. He was beheaded as became a gentleman and a peer, and his epitaph was written a few years later by Edward Hall:

> Many lamented but more rejoiced, and especially such as either had been religious men, or favoured religious persons, for they banqueted and triumphed together that night, many wishing that that day had been seven years before … Others who knew nothing but truth by him both lamented him and heartily prayed for him.[34]

Hall was in no doubt that he had been brought to his death by the 'scoffyng pride' of some prelates who, whatever other causes there may have been, 'did shorten his life and procured the end that he was brought unto'. What Hall did not say was that the king was wholly responsible, but Henry himself knew that, and it was not long before he was regretting his precipitancy.[35]

On the same day that Cromwell met his death, the king married Catherine Howard. Agnes, the Dowager Duchess of Norfolk and Catherine's mentor, later testified that Henry had been smitten with her from the time of their first meeting, which must have been at Greenwich sometime in late December or early January, as she awaited the arrival of her royal mistress. This may have been so, but the first trace of the king's favour which survives of record is a grant dated 24 April to her of the goods and chattels of two murderers who had been executed. In this grant she is simply identified as a servant of Queen Anne,[36] and it does not seem a very romantic kind of gift, but it was an indication of Henry's interest. If the dowager duchess knew of any closer attachment between them, she did not show any sign of it, and she sent a rich gift to the queen on 4 May. During April and May, as we have seen, Anne went on performing her normal duties as queen, and the king dined periodically in her apartments. However, the king's interest in Catherine was growing, and he took to crossing the river to Lambeth for clandestine assignments. These did not take place in the archbishop's palace, however, but almost certainly at Norfolk House, the Duchess's residence, which was close by. Catherine must have gone there specially for that purpose, because she was normally resident at Court, but presumably Henry did not want to encourage gossip by conducting his 'amours' in so public a place. If this was so, the Duchess must have been fully cognisant of what was going on, but unfortunately we do not know when these assignations began, except that they were well established by the time that Anne found out about them on 20 June.[37] Perhaps a gift of two sarcenet quilts from the king on 18 May has some significance in this respect, but probably not. Alarmed, perhaps, by Anne's knowledge of their affair, on 21 or 22 June Catherine withdrew discreetly to Norfolk House, where she seems to have laid low until Henry's intentions were clear. In early July, when the Cleves marriage was on the point of dissolution, and the king had made obvious his plan to replace her with her maid-in-waiting, it was pointed out to Henry that he needed a dispensation because Catherine, as Anne Boleyn's cousin, was within the fourth degree of affinity, and in spite of the Royal Supremacy the traditional canon law was still upheld in England. This, however, Cranmer's Faculty Office was able to supply, and the marriage duly went ahead, as we have seen, on the 28th.[38] Those with an interest in the king's well-being (or an eye on the succession) noted that he was in an ebullient mood, and could barely keep his hands off her. There is no doubt that whatever malfunction he thought that he had been suffering from in his relationship with Anne would not apply to his new queen, which raises an interesting question over her failure to conceive. This cannot have been due to any action on her part, as pregnancy would have sealed their union in the most obvious way, so it must have been that Henry's sexual performance was at best erratic, and at worst non-existent, which would help to explain her subsequent behaviour. Meanwhile, the marriage having been private, she was 'shown to the court' as queen on 8 August.[39] Catherine was a Howard, and it is natural to suppose that her uncle the Duke of Norfolk was in some way behind her rise. He is alleged to have 'dangled' her under the king's nose, but it is hard to see what this means, and harder still to prove. He may have facilitated her trysts with Henry at Norfolk House, and certainly knew about them, but that does not constitute a positive involvement. It is true that Norfolk and Gardiner welcomed her advent as queen, and saw that as a consolidation of the victory which they had won with the execution of Cromwell, but otherwise the initiative seems to have come entirely from the king.[40] That Catherine was a pawn of the Howard faction is a supposition which relies largely on Henry's harsh treatment of the family at the time of her fall. At the time of their wedding, the king was interested in her as a woman, and the fact that she was a Howard was largely incidental. Her family would certainly not have put any obstacles in his way, but more than that cannot be said. Henry had chosen his bride for her personal attractiveness, and it was now up to him to make the most of her – if he could.

5
The Royal Bride

The effect of marriage upon the ageing king was remarkable. He had just passed his forty-ninth birthday, and was showing unmistakable signs of wear and tear. His once magnificent body had run to fat now that he no longer jousted or played tennis, and he had an ulcerated leg, the result of many bruising falls in the tilt-yard and the hunting field. In 1538 these ulcers had closed, causing him exquisite pain, and apparently threatening his very life. He had recovered from that attack, but it had been a sharp reminder of mortality, and when the black humour was on him he had confessed the weight of his age, and had doubted whether he would beget any more children.[1] All that was now forgotten. Instead he adopted 'a new rule of life', rising between five and six in the morning and hunting until dinner at ten, his barrel-like body being no handicap in such an activity, provided that his horses were strong enough. The French ambassador reported that he had never seen him in such good spirits or in so good a humour:

> He tells me that being so much in the country, and changing his place
> [of residence] so often he finds himself in much better health…[2]

During the summer and winter of 1540 this improvement persisted, and he was a picture of well-being; brimming with goodwill and good humour. Any doubts which he might have entertained about his sexual capacity were cast aside in the glow of his new ardour as he caressed his young bride. Nothing was too good for her, and he cherished her with costly gifts and magnificent entertainments, words apparently failing him to describe his devotion. William Thomas declared that she reigned supreme, and in this dreamlike world Catherine soon lost all grasp of reality. Horsham and Lambeth seemed a long way away, and her youthful indiscretions paled into insignificance in the warmth of Henry's affection.

In this situation she became proud and careless. As a Spanish chronicle put it, 'the king had no wife who made him spend so much money on dresses and jewels as she did, who every day had some fresh caprice...'[3] Henry seems to have taken literally his marriage vow to endow his wife with all his worldly goods! Her household was on the same lavish scale, including a chamberlain, chancellor, Master of the Horse, secretary, solicitor and auditor, all appointed by the king, and a variety of lesser positions where her wishes were taken into account. She had four gentleman ushers, two gentleman waiters, a cup bearer, clerks of both her council and her wardrobe, and six chaplains. As a woman, she needed female body servants, and these she seems to have appointed herself – ten ladies, nine attendants, and five maids with their 'mother'. There were also about forty menial servants, who would have been appointed by the chamberlain. It is doubtful if the queen even knew their identities.[4] However some of her chamberers were taken on as a result of direct appeals from former friends of her days in the duchess's household,

Joan Bulmer being a case in point, and employing these young women, as it turned out, was giving hostages to fortune. She was expected, of course, to pay this entourage herself out of her jointure, which was fixed in January 1541 at a similarly generous level. She received not only the lordships and lands which had endowed Jane Seymour, but also a large proportion of the lands of the late Earl of Essex, Thomas Cromwell, of Walter, Lord Hungerford, who had been executed on the same day, and of the abbey of Reading. Altogether her jointure was calculated to return £4,600 a year, which was substantially more than those enjoyed by previous queens, and a mark of the unique affection in which she was then held.[5] This love also manifested itself in the generous gifts of jewels which she received, particularly at Christmas and New Year. These included 'a square containing 27 table diamonds and 26 clusters of pearls'; a brooch constructed of 33 diamonds and 60 rubies with an edge of pearl; and a black velvet muffler furred with sables, containing 38 rubies and no fewer than 572 pearls. In effect she was being presented with the riches of the Tudor treasury by a husband who could only afford such generosity thanks to the dissolution of the abbeys.[6]

Not only was she the recipient of untold wealth, but was entertained almost nightly with banquets and dancing, during which Henry cast off his infirmities, and almost returned to the carefree days of his own youth. When she travelled on the river, she had her own private barge, rowed by twenty-six bargemen and attended by twenty gentlemen 'serving the train'.[7] In return for all this glory, she was expected to receive petitions, and in any matter beyond that modest patronage which was within her gift, to influence her husband in the interest of the petitioner. In this respect she made mistakes, writing directly to Archbishop

Lee of York to request a benefice for her chaplain, Dr Mallet. He could not oblige, as he wrote on 7 December, because he did not grant benefices except on the king's explicit instructions. He also reminded her that, on royal orders, he had promised the next promotion of £40 a year that fell vacant to another of her chaplains, Mr Lowe. She must go through the proper channels.[8] She was also expected to administer her household, oversee the running of her estates, and generally to conduct herself in a meek, sober and submissive fashion. There was no problem with this last requirement, because Catherine did not have a political agenda of her own beyond enhancing the influence of her family, and as early as 3 September Marillac was reporting to Montmorency that she had chosen as her motto *'non aultre volonte que la sienne'* (no other will but his).[9] In respect both of policy and of patronage, she remained true to that profession, largely because she was not interested in anything beyond the trappings of self-adornment. This was no trifling matter, because it involved cosmetics as well as dress, and it was said that a ship could be prepared for the seas in less time than it took a gentlewoman to 'make ready'. The petticoat had to be covered with a bodice and kirtle, farthingale hoops had to be put in place and the whole covered with a gown or cloak. Make up had not yet reached the mask-like excesses which Elizabeth was later to make fashionable, but the ladies of the 1540s adorned their 'face, neck and pappis with ceruse (white lead)' and coloured their cheeks with red ochre or vermilion, producing what has been described as 'a rather garish and artificial effect of peaches and cream'.[10] This was time-consuming and laborious work, and had to be repeated every time that a public appearance was in prospect. It is an open question whether Catherine's beauty needed this kind of enhancement. A few days before her wedding, Marillac wrote to Francis I that 'it is commonly said that the king will marry a lady of great beauty, the daughter of Norfolk's deceased brother…', and that it was his belief that the marriage had already taken place. He was mistaken on this last point, and had clearly never seen Catherine, so his report was by hearsay. When he had made her acquaintance, on 3 September, he revised his opinion. The new queen, he wrote was 'graceful rather than beautiful', and of short stature; although a modern assessment that she was 'plain and dumpy' is probably unfair, it may well have been that she felt in need of cosmetics to enhance her charms.[11] The king did not care and was 'so amorous of her that he cannot treat her well enough…', and on 1 November he added that her ascendancy was so complete that 'the other (Anne) is no longer spoken of'.

Although not entirely without question, Anne's acceptance of her dismissal, and her decision to stay in England, earned Henry's warm approval. On 6 August, two days before Catherine's 'showing' at court, he travelled to Richmond to meet Anne for the first time since their marriage had been annulled. It seems that his visit was motivated mainly by a desire to see for himself that her household arrangements were fully satisfactory, although he may well have been curious to see whether her reported high spirits were genuine or not.[12] She had been faced with a hard choice, because if she had gone back to Cleves there is no doubt that her brother would have tried to arrange another marriage for her, whereas if she stayed in England she could please herself. So family affection had taken second place to the desire to control her own destiny, and she had accepted Henry's generous offer. By then she was in a pensive mood, and her 'joyfulness' was largely simulated, although Henry does not appear to have detected that. At the end of 1540 the court gossips were airing the possibility that she might be reinstated, but the only time that she herself entertained such an ambition was after Catherine's fall over a year later.[13] While her supplanter was in place, she showed her all the respect due to a reigning queen. Henry publicly referred to her as his 'sister', a replacement possibly for Mary, whom he had lost in 1533, and when she visited the court thereafter it was with that status. Her first official visit came in January 1541. She had exchanged New Year gifts with the king, giving him two caparisoned horses, and this invitation may have been in response to that. She travelled to Hampton Court on 3 January, accompanied by Lord William Howard, the queen's uncle, and was welcomed by the Duchess of Suffolk and the Countess of Hertford, who escorted her to Catherine's apartments. Chapuys, who is the source of our information on this encounter, says that Anne greeted the queen on her knees, and was shown 'great kindness' by her. The king had then come in, bowed to Lady Anne and kissed her. The three of them had then dined together, and when the king had withdrawn Anne and Catherine had danced together.[14] The following day they repeated this performance, and the impression given was one of perfect harmony, which is more than could be said for the queen's relations with Princess Mary, who (again according to Chapuys), had snubbed her and been rewarded with the removal of two of her waiting women. In reporting this incident on 5 December 1540 the ambassador expressed the view that the king had forced a reconciliation upon them, and that the two maids would remain in post. This incident (if it ever happened) does not seem in any way to have impaired Henry's affection for his wife.[15]

There were rocks, however, beneath the apparently smooth surface of this connubial harmony. The king's Indian summer was a shallow phenomenon, because in spite of all pretence, his energy was running down. He could still hunt between mass and dinner, but no longer spend all day in the saddle; he could still cut a nimble caper, but no longer dance all night. His reserves of stubborn determination were remarkable, but could not disguise the fact that he was not the man he had been, and needed to be to please his youthful wife. Throughout the autumn of 1540 there were persistent rumours that she was pregnant, but it was not so, and in spite of his uxoriousness, it may be supposed that Henry was no longer a satisfactory lover. Either that or the rumours, which began to circulate in the following year, that she was barren had some substance in fact. In any case her failure to conceive in the autumn of 1540 was a big disappointment to the king, to her kindred and no doubt to Catherine herself.[16] Henry's health was also not as 'well amended' as he liked to claim. His game leg necessitated the use of a walking stick, and he suffered from occasional chronic headaches and attacks of gout. These attacks 'sharpened [his] accustomed patience', and made him increasingly difficult to deal with as the months went by. It was noted that he was often of a different opinion in the morning and after dinner, which made life difficult for his council and impossible for his wife. He also began to evince a nervous restlessness, ceaselessly moving between Westminster and Windsor, Greenwich and Richmond. He might argue that changing residences in the country was good for his health, but these removals were something else, and taxed the resources of the royal household to the limit.[17] It was obvious to everyone except Henry himself that these constant changes of air were doing nothing to stave off the onset of old age. Catherine may have married a semi-divine king, but he was also a man grown fat and fretful. It soon became obvious that not even her most winning ways would provide immunity from his fickle moods – to say nothing of his violent passions. Then in March 1541, the ulcer on his leg closed up again, and it was thought for about a week that the king would die. He recovered, but the dream of renewed youth, which his marriage to Catherine had seemed to promise, died instead. It was said of him that apart from his bodily ailments he had a *'mal d'esprit'*, and nothing was able to please him. For upwards of a month he declined to see his wife, to her great distress, because she could not think what she might have done to displease him.[18] The answer was nothing; but that did not relieve her mind. He grumbled at his council for persuading him to get rid of Cromwell, and complained that he had 'an unhappy people to govern', threatening that he would shortly make them all too poor to resist him. So depressed was he that he spent Shrovetide, which should have been a time for music and entertainments, sulking in his tent without dancing or company, and Catherine was constrained to spend the last few days before Lent in an atmosphere of unaccustomed piety.[19] When he emerged from this black fit, the king took to alternating between moods of introverted nagging about his ailments and vigorous bursts of energy, which taxed his hapless wife even further. Now that she was back in his presence, Catherine discovered that he needed both a doll and a sick nurse, and although she was temperamentally well-suited to play the pampered and irresponsible child, the role of companion was completely beyond her. She simply lacked the intellectual and moral resources for such a position.

Instead she was in constant need of reassurance when it came to her own position, and inclined to become tearful if ignored. Not long before their northern progress in the summer of 1541, she fell into one of these gloomy moods, and when Henry enquired the reason, she replied that it was on account of the rumours circulating that he was going to take back Anne of Cleves as his wife. Whether these reports were real or existed only in her own imagination is not clear, but it took his reassurance of his undying affection to restore her to a good humour.[20] Part of the reason for this insecurity was the fact that she had not been crowned. Although she had been proclaimed as queen, and included in the prayers for the royal family, she remained queen consort only. The reason for this is not clear. Both Catherine of Aragon and Anne Boleyn had been crowned, but it could be argued that there was a political point to be made in each case, and that Jane Seymour, about whom there was no point to be made, was not. It may be simply that Henry did not see the need to crown a wife of whom he was clearly so fond, but the suspicion lingers that had she become pregnant, a Coronation would have soon followed. Following the birth of Prince Edward, Jane would undoubtedly have been crowned had she lived, and it is natural to suppose that if Catherine had produced a son, she would have been dealt with in the same fashion. The French ambassador noted in April 1541 that the queen 'was thought to be with child, which would be a very great joy to this king, who, it seems, believes it, and intends, if it be found true, to have her crowned at Whitsuntide'.[21] To Marillac at any rate, the connection between pregnancy and coronation was clearly established. Also, although there was no good reason to believe it, it was widely held that an uncrowned queen was easier to get rid of, and that in a sense, Catherine was on probation until she had borne a child. Anne or no Anne, it was generally suspected that if she did not bear at least a daughter in the fairly near future, Catherine would be in danger of being repudiated as Anne had been, only on grounds of infertility rather than non-consummation. Nor was her security enhanced by the fact that she remained very much a Howard, and although it is probably not true to say that she owed her position partly to her uncle's influence, he nevertheless expected to benefit from it. The removal of Thomas Cromwell had left the way clear for conservative forces to dominate both in the court and in the council, and the Duke of Norfolk expected his voice to be heard in policy decisions. His colleague (and in a sense rival) the Bishop of Winchester had regained his seat on the council from which Cromwell had temporarily succeeded in expelling him. The omens were favourable. Robert Ratcliffe, Earl of Sussex, his old ally and relation by marriage, succeeded the Earl of Essex as Lord Great Chamberlain and William FitzWilliam, the Earl of Southampton, had taken over as Lord Privy Seal.[22] Thomas Audley, Anthony Browne and Thomas Wriothesley, who had all been appointed under Cromwell had made their peace with the conservatives, and Norfolk and Sussex between them controlled access to the king's patronage. This was where Catherine came in, because her access to Henry was unique, and her ability to promote petitions to him correspondingly great. She also filled (and persuaded Henry to fill) many of the positions in her household with Howard friends and relations. Everyone who had a claim on the new queen, either of blood or of gratitude, and everyone who could claim through friendship, kindred or service a right to Howard patronage, now looked for the golden time. Even the family tailor said, while the outcome was still uncertain, that 'if she were advanced, he expected a good living', and there is no reason to suppose that he was disappointed.[23] As we have seen, Joan Bulmer, a friend from the dodgy days at Horsham, solicited and obtained a place in the queen's Privy Chamber. Under pressure from her uncle, she was unable to say no to any of these suppliants, and the king was in the mood to gratify her whims in the early days of their marriage. So the Howard patronage network spread throughout the court. Three of the six ladies of her chamber were members of the family, her sister Isabel Baynton being one of them, while Isabel's husband, Sir Edward, became governor of her household. Apart from Joan Bulmer, three other friends from the duchess's household became her chamberers, and her aunt, Lady Margaret Arundel, was also in attendance. Meanwhile the grants and favours bestowed upon other relations became very numerous. Her brother George became a gentleman of the Privy Chamber, and with his brother Charles received a licence to import 1,000 tuns of Gascon wine without paying any duty on them, a concession worth over £100. Charles was appointed to the Band of Gentlemen Pensioners, with a fee of £50 a year, and uncle William Howard received gowns and jackets from the royal wardrobe.[24] Lady Baynton was given a present of £100 for no very obvious reason, and other gifts could be cited. Catherine also succeeded, at the duke's request, in persuading Henry to give the French embassy to his brother William, which says a great deal about their relative positions in the power structure of the court.

She also seems to have played the merciful lady to some effect. Although no opportunity arose to match those given to Catherine of Aragon and the king's sister Mary by the Evil May Day of 1517, when 400 offenders were released by their intercessions, she nevertheless succeeded in saving the life of a certain Helen Page, due to be executed for murder, and rescued her cousin John Legh from consignment to the Tower on a charge of treason. She also seems to have intervened on behalf of the poet, Sir Thomas Wyatt, when his indiscretions seemed likely to provoke the royal wrath. In spite of her lack of political awareness, or even intelligence, her part in the structure of Howard influence at court was very great by the summer of 1541, and that inevitably meant that she attracted the hostility and envy of those outside the charmed circle. Those who resented the Howard ascendancy now had a target who might prove more vulnerable than the duke, because she was quite without imagination, and seems to have been unable to grasp the extent to which she was now surrounded by vicious political intrigue.[25] Although in the ascendant for the time being, Howard influence was by no means secure, because the remains of Thomas Cromwell's party lurked, particularly in the Privy Chamber, and had taken heart at Henry's discontented words in March 1541, when he had denounced his councillors for having allowed him to destroy 'the best servant that ever he had'. Marillac saw the danger, but also the advantage to his master, writing that 'as long as they are making war on each other, they will innovate nothing against France'.[26] The reformers were down, but by no means out, and the Evangelicals nursed a bitter hatred for the Howards and all their supporters. John Lascelles, who was eventually to denounce Catherine's infidelities, was one such. At the time of the Howard marriage, being informed that the devil was triumphant at court, he is alleged to have said 'be not too rash in maintaining the Scriptures' for the enemies of God would shortly destroy themselves. Whether this was sheer optimism, or whether he already had some idea of the tidings which he would eventually bring, it was nevertheless a very prescient remark.[27] Unfortunately for Catherine, she seems never to have inspired that personal loyalty, which was very necessary for one in her position. Jane Seymour had been much loved, and even Anne Boleyn had attracted a good deal of personal loyalty, but Catherine seems to have been surrounded by malice. This may have been one reason why she filled her household with members of the family, who would at least be kind to her out of gratitude, but the fact is that her role as queen depended entirely upon Henry for its continuance – just as Cromwell's had done. Just as he had had servants but no friends, so Catherine had dependants, but no one outside her extended clan upon whom she could rely if things started to go wrong.

The potential for that to happen was there all the while, because Henry had assumed that his bride was a chaste virgin, and she had understandably not disabused him. Her affairs with Henry Mannox, and more seriously with Francis Dereham were not exactly secret; her 'bedfellows' knew of them, and so (probably) did the dowager duchess, but the king did not, and it was at that stage not in anyone's interests to tell him.[28] Instead her friends used their knowledge to infiltrate themselves into her household, where their secrecy was the price of continue favour. When Catherine had departed from Horsham in December 1539 to take up her place in Anne of Cleves' household, Dereham had been left behind in the duchess's service. He tried unsuccessfully to get released, and then in January took himself off to Ireland without either warning or permission. The dowager spread the story that he had left of a broken heart after Catherine had rejected him, but the true reason for his departure seems to have been that he decided to try his hand at a little piracy.[29] If that was the reason, then it clearly did not work because he was back in London by the late spring of 1540. He had not bothered to tell Catherine of his plans, and she had no idea of his whereabouts until he suddenly reappeared. He similarly was not aware of the changes which had taken place in her circumstances. She was no longer the dowager's ward, a girl with whom a young man of birth but no particular prospects might safely dally. Instead she was at the centre of the court, and an attraction to a swarm of eligible suitors. Among these, two appeared to be particularly successful: Thomas Paston and Thomas Culpepper, both gentlemen of the king's Privy Chamber, and indeed rumour had it that the latter was betrothed to her and that the pair would shortly marry.[30] Dereham, however, was not disposed to give way, and kept up his suit in spite of Catherine's blunt warning that he was wasting his time. When the king began to show a serious interest in her, like Culpepper he effaced himself and did not appear at court for a number of months, because it was not becoming (or safe) for a mere gentleman to compete with his sovereign, no matter how smitten he was with the lady. He was, however, unwise enough to remark after the royal wedding that if the king were dead 'I am sure I might marry her', which constituted the treasonable offence of 'imagining the king's death' in accordance with the statute of 1534.[31]

He returned to the court, bizarrely enough, on the intercession of the Duchess of Norfolk, who requested Catherine to find a position for him. He was something of a favourite with the dowager, who showed no inclination to punish him for his unauthorised departure earlier in the year, but if she was aware of the true state of their earlier relationship, then she was taking an appalling risk. Perhaps she simply did not believe that he would be foolish enough to continue his sexual pursuit of a woman who was now the queen. Catherine responded favourably to her grandmother's request, and asked the dowager to bring Dereham with her next time that she visited the court, which she did, probably for the Christmas festivities of 1540–1.[32] The queen gave him money, and must have found a place for him in her household, because he remained behind when the duchess departed, and seems to have been already in Catherine's service when he was promoted to be her private secretary in August 1541. It looks like sheer adolescent folly to give a former lover this kind of privileged access, but neither the dowager nor her daughter Lady Bridgewater saw anything wrong with it. In their eyes it was perfectly proper for Catherine to bestow her patronage on old friends in such a fashion, and they were not to know that he would be foolish enough to throw his weight about on the strength of an intimacy which should never have existed.[33] It may well be that some of the boasts later attributed to him were invented for the purpose, but he must have done something to arouse the antagonism of his fellow courtiers to the point where they were inclined to make such fabrications. He is alleged to have said that he was of the queen's council before his interlocutor knew her, and would be there 'after she hath forgotten him'.[34] It may have been remarks of this kind that Catherine had in mind when she warned him to beware what words he spoke. If so, her wisdom was greater than his, but not even the most indiscreet of his remarks suggested a renewed sexual relationship, and it is reasonably certain that there that there was none. However Catherine's romantic desire to play the Lady Bountiful had betrayed her into a rash association, and as the great northern progress of 1541 approached, she had given another hostage to fortune.

Thomas Cromwell had no successor, and the council in which Norfolk and his allies played a dominant part was responsible directly to the king. So Henry must have authorised the executions which took place on 30 July, just two days after his minister's death and his own wedding, when three of Cromwell's dependants went to the stake at Smithfield.[35] Like him they had been condemned by Act of Attainder, so that parliament had assumed the role of the supreme spiritual court of the realm; the only occasion upon which it was to do so. The charge against them was of Anabaptism, so that their fate has to be seen as part of that web of conspiracy which had brought down the Lord Privy Seal. In fact their main crime seems to have been to offend Stephen Gardiner, because Barnes had made a personal attack upon him in a sermon at Paul's Cross, and Jerome and Garrett had supported him. The three of them had been brought before the king and had recanted, whereupon they were required to prove their orthodoxy in sermons at St Mary Spital in Easter week. This they had duly done, but not to Gardiner's satisfaction, who 'by his privy complaining to the king' contrived to get the three of them committed to the Tower.[36] However the real reason for their fall lay not in their doctrine, which was largely Lutheran, but in the need to discredit Cromwell by association. The charges were manifestly fabricated, and they did not know why they were condemned to death, a point which Barnes made abundantly clear in his final oration. He denied that he had ever been an Anabaptist, and claimed that all his 'study and diligence' had been to refute their errors – which was true. He was condemned to die 'but wherefore I cannot tell', and the sheriff who presided was unable to enlighten him. The case with the others was the same, and they went to their deaths in a fog of incomprehension,

the victims of their close association with Thomas Cromwell, and
of the conservative need to 'cleanse the stables' before insisting
upon their own brand of orthodoxy.[37] At the same time three
further victims were executed for 'popish treason' at Tyburn.
These men, Edward Powell, Richard Featherstone and Thomas
Abel, were at least in no doubt as to why they were to die, and
were guilty as charged, but the need to despatch them is no
clearer. Probably their deaths were needed by Gardiner and his
associates to stave off any charges of Roman sympathies which
might be levelled against them in the wake of the destruction
of Cromwell, because they knew that the latter's friends were
not eradicated, and the king's favour was not to be relied upon.
Whether Henry was really concentrating when he signed the
death warrants of these men may be doubted, but he was no
doubt sufficiently content to see the executions as representing a
balanced policy for the independence of his church.[38] Meanwhile
the king had decided to honour his new-found youthfulness by
resuming his military career. As early as February 1540 he had
sent Sir Ralph Sadler on a mission to Scotland, in an effort to
persuade his nephew James V to follow his example in dealing
with the Court of Rome. Sadler's instructions were patronising in
tone and would not have been delivered as set, but the object was
to offer English aid 'to bring his good determination to a perfect
end and conclusion'.[39] This was probably because he envisaged
a new Imperial alliance in the wake of his freshly established
religious credentials, and realised that this would eventually
mean war with France. Remembering what had happened in
1513, he was therefore anxious to neutralise the Scots in advance,
and sought to do this by urging the merits of the royal supremacy
upon James. However the King of Scots was not to be drawn. He

already had enough control over the church in his dominions for his purposes, and most of the richer abbeys were in the hands of lay commendators, so he had no incentive to upset the pope.[40] Sadler's mission was therefore a failure, and over a year later Henry wrote again, this time directly to James, upbraiding him for being so influenced by 'kirkmen' and suggesting that they meet at York during his forthcoming progress to the north, to resolve their differences and hopefully to find a common way forward. However, James's infant son had died in the spring of 1541, and his council was adamantly opposed to the risk involved in any journey to the south. The Scottish king, did not make this clear to his uncle, who set off in June 1541 fully expecting to meet James in York.[41] His chagrin when this did not happen was correspondingly great, and small-scale military activity along the border was stepped up. If he was unable to tempt James by friendship, a spot of intimidation might not come amiss. By the time that the king set out for the north, the black humour which had possessed him in March was apparently forgotten, and in spite of his ailments he was in fine fettle, and in an aggressive mood, both towards Scotland and towards France. Marillac noticed that his Imperial rival was getting most of the attention, and blamed the Howards.

6
The Progress of 1541

At the end of June 1541 Henry set out on his long-anticipated journey to York. Never before had the court migrated on such a scale or with such magnificence. Apart from the 500 or so members of his household, the king was accompanied by an escort of 1,000 soldiers, and 5,000 horses were needed for mounts and transport. Because many of the places where they would be staying would be too small to house this army, 200 tents were taken along as well and the escort was equipped with a number of field guns.[1] It resembled, as one historian has observed, an army of occupation rather than a royal tour. The reason for this was that Henry was by no means sure of his welcome. Not only was there still grumbling resentment in some quarters following the suppression of the Pilgrimage of Grace five years earlier, there had been a minor conspiracy as recently as April, when a group of malcontents had endeavoured to use the Spring Fair at Pontefract to raise a standard of revolt. However, only 300 or so had actually turned up, and thanks to advance information the council had been able to nip this revolt in the bud.[2] It was not sufficient to deter the king, but it was a warning that proper precautions should be taken. It was also sufficient to seal the fate of the sixty-eight-year-old Countess of Salisbury, who had been languishing in the Tower since 1538. She might eventually have been pardoned if it had not been for this manifestation of discontent. Progresses were a necessary part of the display pattern of the monarchy, because they enabled the ruler to appear before his subjects in person, and to deal with their requests and grievances directly. They were also helpful in overawing potential opposition by the sheer scale of their splendour, and Henry had never been north of Boston before. So a visit to Yorkshire was long overdue, and he came accompanied by his richest tapestries, his finest plate and his most sumptuous clothes. He also came with his queen, and her ceremonial attire complemented his own, completing the royal presence. She was expected to intercede for suppliants, and to mitigate the royal wrath, should that be required.[3]

Unfortunately the weather was vile, with constant rain and high winds making the roads almost impassable. It took the vast procession nearly three weeks to reach Grafton, and at Liddington on the way the queen became unwell. Her indisposition was not serious, and does not seem to have further impeded such progress as had been made. They stopped at Grimesthorpe, the Duke of Suffolk's residence in south Lincolnshire, and reached Lincoln on 9 August.[4] The rain held off, and their entry to the town was carefully choreographed. Preceded by eighty archers and by the principal officers of state, the royal couple were followed by the king's 'horse of state', with all its trappings, by a group of local children dressed for the occasion in cloth of gold and crimson velvet, and by the ladies and gentlemen of the court in their finest array. The citizens had spent weeks decorating their town with pennants, badges, escutcheons, and with pageants commemorating Tudor triumphs, particularly over the Scots. At the gates they were met by the mayor and assembled worthies, who presented the king with the sword and keys of the city, as symbols of their joyful submission.[5] Meanwhile the bells of all the churches rang out, and the king made his way to the cathedral to give thanks for having come safely thus far, and for the welcome which he had received. In order to make sure that the inexperienced locals got their greetings right, a knowledgeable courtier had been sent in advance to advise them; and his efforts can be seen not only at Lincoln, but also in Northamptonshire, at Peterborough and at Stamford, where the town mace was duly presented before the king as the token of submission. On 24 August he arrived at Pontefract, where Sir John Neville had so recently attempted to base his rising, and on 18 September he reached York, where the old abbey of St Mary's had been refurbished to receive him. There he awaited the arrival of his nephew the King of Scots, and the Duke of Norfolk, who had acted as harbinger, could relax with the thought of a job well done.[6]

Henry had so far been on good form, cheerful and magnanimous. He had been entertained on his way north with periodic hunting trips, and these had been particularly well received. At Hatfield no fewer than 200 stags and does had been slaughtered in an extravagant orgy which probably involved the wretched animals being corralled in the park and driven past the king, rather than in his active pursuit. It is hard to see him despatching more than a tenth of that number in an orthodox chase. On another occasion he presided over the destruction of a great quantity of young swans, and filled two boats with waterfowl and fish.

Such slaughter could be justified on the ground that the king and his entourage needed to be kept supplied with fresh game and fish, but that was not the real reason for it. Henry needed to be kept amused, and the Duke of Suffolk's main activity during the progress was to organise these hunts, which seem to have happened at every stopping point.[7] More than this was needed, however, to keep the king in a good humour. Protocol had to be very strictly observed. We have seen how carefully he was received at Lincoln, and when he reached York he was separately presented with two very different groups of gentlemen. Once the formalities of his reception were completed, those who had been loyal to him during the Pilgrimage were granted an audience, during which the king thanked them and bestowed generous favours. Then those who had been less loyal, but had escaped direct punishment were brought in. They knelt and prostrated themselves, while their spokesman intoned:

> ...we wretches, for lack of grace and of sincere and pure knowledge of the verity of God's words have most grievously, heinously and wantonly offended your Majesty in the unnatural and most odious and detestable offences of outrageous disobedience and traitorous rebellion...[8]

For this they humbly begged his forgiveness. They accompanied their supplication with a sizeable purse of money, and Henry pronounced himself graciously satisfied. In both cases these were ritual acts of royal benevolence, and would have been understood as such. He also had good reason to be satisfied, because everywhere on his way north he had been greeted with evidence of goodwill and with handsome hospitality. The fact that these demonstrations had been carefully planned in advance did not make them any less gratifying. The one thing that was not gratifying was the non-appearance of the King of Scots. The elaborate preparations at St Mary's Abbey, which had kept hundreds of men busy for several weeks, had been wasted and Henry was not pleased. His good humour rapidly evaporated and he set out for the south again on 29 September in a foul temper, feeling (and saying) that he had been mocked by his nephew.[9] Reprisals were in his mind. The weather was kinder this time, and the need for display and amusements less, so that the journey which had taken two and a half months on the way out, took only about three weeks coming back. By the end of October he was back at Westminster.

Publicly, the queen was his loyal companion in all these activities, but they were not regularly sleeping together, and Catherine was feeling romantically deprived. She solaced herself with Thomas Culpepper, who, as we have seen, had been tipped to marry her before the king came on the scene. In the spring of 1541 Henry had shut his wife out of his life, and it may have been at that time that Culpepper reappeared. In a sense, as a gentleman of the Privy Chamber, he had never gone away, but they had discreetly kept their distance from each other until shortly before the progress began.[10] It was clear by then that Henry was a most unsatisfactory lover. He was not impotent, but his performance was very erratic, and Catherine became increasingly frustrated. She was young and needed a youthful mate, not this ageing and corpulent man, who was periodically in such pain that all romantic thoughts were banished. When the king was in a good mood, he desired his wife, as all the commentators noticed, but when he was sick or out of humour, he did not; and that was no basis for a stable relationship. When she began to see Thomas privately we do not know, but it seems to have been at Greenwich before the progress commenced. They exchanged rings, and went through other rituals of the game of courtly love, and if it had remained at that level, no harm might have ensued.[11] However, Catherine was plainly smitten with this attractive young man, and as the progress developed they commenced a series of secret trysts, probably meeting at every place where the court stopped, although that is not clear. The queen's chief gentlewoman, Jane Rochford, was a party to all this clandestine activity. She carried messages between them, and sought out suitable spots for the couple to meet at each stopping place. At Liddington, during the queen's indisposition in late July, and again at Grimesthorpe she had exchanged secret letters with Catherine the purport of which was that she should have 'that thing which was promised her' which appears to have been a secret rendezvous with Culpepper.[12] The impression given is that Jane was actively promoting the affair, but that was probably not the case. She was, however, in the habit of investigating the possibility of back-stairs access to the queen's apartments. This was particularly successful at Lincoln, because although their stay was only three nights, the couple were able to meet on two of them.[13] They were taking an incredible risk because Jane was not the only one of Catherine's attendants to notice that there was something going on. Katherine Tilney observed that the queen was 'out of her chamber when it was late'. She was in fact in Jane Rochford's room, which was conveniently situated close by, with Thomas Culpepper. It was after two in the morning when she eventually went to bed in her own room. Culpepper later denied that they had done anything other than talk, but the fact was that he had arrived about eleven o'clock and not departed until nearly three. It is not surprising that suspicions should have been aroused.[14] He had been lucky to gain access at all that night, because when Jane had been looking out for him, the watchman had appeared and had locked the door. Jane had made herself scarce, and when Culpepper turned up shortly after he was obliged to get a resourceful servant to pick the lock. Katherine Tilney was not the only person to be aware of these secret assignations. The following night he came again, and this time Jane, who was present at their meeting, conveniently fell asleep at some distance from the loving couple, and so did not notice what transpired between them.[15]

At Pontefract this could have resulted in disaster because Catherine had by this time taken to bolting her chamber door on the inside, and when Anthony Denny of the Privy Chamber turned up one evening to summon her to the king, he was unable to gain access. Presumably this difficulty was overcome and Denny was admitted, because Henry certainly was not informed of any glitch, and did not notice anything amiss in his relations with his wife.[16] Nevertheless the queen became nervous, and by the time that they got to York was convinced that the king was setting a setting a 'privy watch' on her. Jane persuaded a maidservant of her own to keep watch, but she detected nothing unusual, and Culpepper came as he was accustomed to do that night, remaining with her until a late hour. Again he claimed that they were just talking and Jane positioned herself at a safe distance so that she could truthfully claim that she did not know what had transpired. But Thomas, like the queen, was nervous by this time, and spent quite a lot of his tryst hovering on the stairs in case he should be required to beat a hasty retreat. At

York he gave Catherine a ring, and received a pair of bracelets in return, while she teased him about all the other lovers she could have had if she had been so inclined.[17] The affair seems to have lasted throughout the rest of the progress, but nothing particularly notable happened on the way back, and the nerves of all concerned must have become quieter. The letters which were exchanged between Jane Rochford and Catherine were all destroyed, probably at the time, but one letter does survive, which seems to have been written in August 1541 after the stop at Lincoln. It is by Catherine, and addressed to Thomas Culpepper. It starts sedately enough; 'Master Culpepper I commend me to you, praying you to send me word how you do...', but then becomes more animated. She had heard that he was sick and never longed so much for anything as to see him. 'It makes my heart die to think that I cannot be always in your company. Come when my Lady Rochford is here...', and she signed herself 'yours as long as life endures, Katheryn'.[18] It is unmistakeably a love letter, and he presumably kept it for that reason, although it was a foolish thing to do. The question of Jane Rochford's role in all this remains uncertain, because she claimed to be always acting under the queen's instructions, while Catherine claimed that she was an active pander. While she was under interrogation later in the year, the queen understandably alleged that Jane had constantly urged her to infidelity with Culpepper, and that she had resisted such pressure. All their long and numerous sessions together had resulted in mere talk, a prolonged flirtation without any consummation. He concurred, although he admitted a desire to 'do the deed' with her, and believed that that desire was mutual.[19] For her part Jane Rochford believed that coitus had taken place, although she was unable to say where or when, possibly because of her convenient habit of falling asleep. Francis Dereham may have nurtured similar ambitions, but he realised that he had been supplanted in the queen's affections, and did not at this time do anything to disturb them. What is more remarkable in view of the number of servants who must have been at least partly privy to what was going on, is that no one thought of informing the king, who went through the entire progress with Catherine at his side, going about their public responsibilities, without a suspicion of what was going on almost literally under his nose.

Jane Boleyn, Viscountess Rochford, was clearly a key player in this game of courtly love, and it is worth remembering who she was, and why she might have been willing to play the pander in the manner alleged. She had been born in about 1505, the second child but eldest daughter of Henry Parker, Lord Morley, and of Alice, his wife, the daughter of Sir John St John of Bletso.[20] After the conventional early training of an aristocratic girl, she had been introduced to the court, somewhere in the lower reaches of Queen Catherine's household. There, at the age of about thirteen or fourteen she had first played the game of courtly love, flirting conventionally with the young gallants. She was, however, strictly chaperoned, and would have learned early on that these games had nothing to do with real love, which remained forbidden territory. She accompanied the queen to the Field of Cloth of Gold in 1520, but first emerges into the light of history with her part in the defence of the Château Vert in 1522, that magnificent entertainment provided for the visiting emperor, which indicates that she was considered to be one of the more presentable members of the court.[21] Meanwhile she was of a suitable age, and her father began to turn his thoughts to the question of her marriage. There is no sign that Jane was consulted in this process, but by 1523 Lord Morley was in discussion with Sir Thomas Boleyn about the prospects of a match with his only son George. The Boleyns were near neighbours of the Parkers, and George had been at court for a number of years, so the chances are that the young couple knew each other reasonably well. In 1524 the negotiations were completed, Lord Morley agreeing a jointure of £1,300, towards which the king, interestingly, made a significant contribution, indicating his approval of the arrangement. George was undoubtedly one of his favourites, and about three months before the papers were finally signed, he granted the young man the manor of Grimstone to provide a family home for the couple when they were not at court.[22] The jointure was agreed on 4 October 1524, and the chances are that the marriage took place either in November 1524 or very early in 1525.

In spite of the splendours of the wedding, and the ritual bedding which followed it, it does not appear to have been a very successful union. Jane did not become pregnant, and the couple continued to spend most of their time at court, lodged as a married couple on the king's side. George also lost his privileged position in the king's Privy Chamber as a result of Wolsey's reorganisation of the household in May 1525.[23] It is not known why, but with Mary Boleyn married to William Carey, who retained his place, Henry might well have felt that he had enough Boleyns about him. Sir Thomas was raised to the peerage as Viscount Rochford in 1525, and when he became Earl of Wiltshire in October 1529, George received the honorific title of Rochford, and Jane became a viscountess. By 1529 George's sister Anne occupied a unique place in the royal affections, and the influence of her kindred seemed secure. Consequently

Jane's life did not turn out as expected. Instead of spending the majority of her time on the Boleyn estates, punctuated by occasional visits to the court, or back to Great Hallingbury to see her parents, and instead of the children which she could reasonably have expected, she found herself a lady-in-waiting to the new queen.[24] Meanwhile in 1528 George and Anne had both contracted the sweat, that dreaded influenza-like disease which carried off thousands in that fraught summer. Henry panicked and wrote anguished letters to his beloved, but declined to allow her anywhere near the court. William Carey succumbed to the illness, but both Anne and George recovered, and Jane seems to have escaped altogether. When Anne returned to duty, her sister-in-law was at her side, and there she seems to have remained as Anne's fortunes waxed after 1529. George may well have been involved in Wolsey's fall in the autumn of that year; he was by then a member of the council and active in support of his father, but his wife was not and we have no idea of her reaction to the great minister's demise. It was none of her business. She took part in Anne's coronation in June 1533, enjoyed her stipend as a lady of the Privy Chamber, and was well in favour without making herself conspicuous.[25] She also shared in George's good fortune, as he received grants from the king in the form of lands and remunerative offices. However the years passed; children did not come, and her husband appears to have consoled himself with other women. That George Boleyn who became Dean of Lichfield in 1576 is alleged to have been his bastard son, but the name of his mother is not known.[26] Viscount Rochford also spent a fair amount if time on diplomatic missions, which means that Jane would have been quite accustomed to being on her own. Whether she was barren, or their sex life was in some way unsatisfactory, we do not know, but it was most unusual for a woman to be married for ten years and not to have undergone a single pregnancy. Something was wrong because George had a reputation as a ladies' man; the idea that he was homosexual is quite without foundation. Anne, however, failed to produce the son which the king so desperately needed. The birth of Elizabeth in September 1533 was followed by miscarriages in 1534 and 1536, and Henry's demons re-awoke. His relationship with his wife, which had always been physical in its nature, became fitful without ceasing to be passionate, and by April 1536 it had turned sour. The first sign that something might be wrong occurred when George failed to be elected to the Order of the Garter on the 23rd. The king preferred Sir Nicholas Carew, who was in the Seymour camp, and Jane Seymour was lurking in the wings of the king's favour, ready to take over should Anne fall from grace.[27] Chapuys was delighted by this evidence of declining Boleyn influence. The queen, he chuckled, did not even have sufficient influence to get her own brother knighted. Within a week she had been arrested and taken to the Tower.

Anne's fall was the subject of much salacious speculation at the time, and has remained controversial ever since, but there is no doubt that the key player was Thomas Cromwell. While the Boleyns were locked in battle with the followers of Catherine of Aragon, Cromwell had allied with them, but it was an alliance of convenience, not marked by any real friendship, and when Catherine died in January 1536, the situation changed. Cromwell was in favour of rebuilding Henry's relations with the emperor, and to that policy the Francophile Boleyns (and particularly Anne) were vehemently opposed.[28] When the king began to blow hot and cold on his relationship with his queen, Cromwell saw his chance. By removing Anne he would not only clear an obstacle from his political path, he would also get rid of rivals for Henry's favour. He realised that Anne was no mean politician, and that he could not simply shunt her into retirement as Catherine had been shunted. She would need to be eliminated, and, given the go-ahead by the king to conduct the investigation, he set out to build up a case of criminal adultery, which would ensure her execution, and that of any other members of her family who could be swept into the net.[29] George, who seems to have been quite unaware that there was anything seriously wrong, was arrested within hours of his sister, and likewise lodged in the Tower. A bewildered Jane was summoned before the council for questioning. By the time that that happened, Cromwell already had a fat dossier of statements and confessions from other members of the Privy Chamber, and a number of incriminating statements from Anne herself. In confinement and surrounded by unsympathetic people, she had babbled inconsequentially, particularly of her conversation with Henry Norris the day before she was arrested. Surprised by his failure to 'come on' to Madge Shelton, whom Anne had earmarked for him, and by his statement of courtly love to the effect that he loved only his queen, she had accused him of waiting for dead men's shoes 'if any harm should come to the king'.[30] Such a statement was treasonable, and they both knew it. Moreover, unknown to Jane was the fact that Mark Smeaton had already confessed to intercourse with Anne, although how or when that had come about was not clear. Cromwell's questioning of Lady Rochford had therefore concentrated on the queen's relations with George. How often did they meet? Who else was present on those occasions? Was he ever alone with her? These, and a remorseless series of other questions focussed on aspects of

Anne's sexual life, were pressed upon her as she did her best to satisfy her inquisitors. She was forced to confess that the queen was often alone with her brother, but she had no idea what they talked about. Maliciously interpreted, this could be construed as evidence of sexual malpractice, and the charges of incest against George were largely based on Jane's statements, which actually said no such thing.[31] In spite of the construction which was placed upon her words, Jane had no intention of harming her husband. Indeed if he were convicted of treason she would be left penniless apart from her jointure, so she had every incentive to support him. She sent him a message, promising to plead with the king for him, which encouraged him a good deal, but she never got a chance to do so. Thomas Cromwell had total control of access to the king, and had no intention of allowing one his prime suspects to escape. George was duly tried and, along with his sister, was convicted and executed. At the age of thirty-one, Jane was a widow.

All that George had owned, by virtue of his attainder now belonged to the king. His possessions and those of his wife were meticulously inventoried, and his confiscated to the king's use. His lands and offices reverted to the crown, and all that Jane was left with was her jointure of 100 marks (£66) a year.[32] Lord Morley was reluctant to get involved, so she took the only course open to her and appealed to Thomas Cromwell for aid. She may have felt that he owed her something for her evidence, which had been used in the trials, but it was not wise to trust to the minister's gratitude. Instead she wrote a humble beseeching letter describing herself as a 'poor desolate widow without comfort', begging Cromwell to approach the king for her. She sought the return of George's 'stuff', and the amelioration of her jointure, reminding him that the king had been a generous contributor to the original arrangement, but that now she found it very hard to 'shift in the world' on 100 marks a year.[33] All that she could offer in return was her prayers and service. Henry did not respond directly, but he leant on the Earl of Wiltshire, in exile from the court after the disgrace of his children, to improve her jointure to £100 a year. This he duly did, and increased the allowance which she was to receive from his estate after his death from 200 marks to 300. Jane now had a measure of security, but her dazzling days at court were apparently over.[34] She could either wait in obscurity in the hope that Lord Morley would make another marriage for her, or she could petition Cromwell again for a place in the household of the new queen, Jane Seymour, whom Henry had married within a month of Anne's execution. Just how quickly he responded we do not know, but within few months Jane Rochford was back in the familiar environment of the queen's apartments. There was, however, one big difference. Then she had been the sister-in-law of the queen and the wife of a well-regarded courtier. Now she was the widow of a convicted traitor and adulterer, whose name could not be spoken within the precincts of the court. Although reinstated, she was very much on her own.

Meanwhile, Cromwell needed an agent on the queen's side, not least to keep an eye on the activities of the Seymour brothers, Edward and Thomas, and Jane had offered him her service. He could not wander into the queen's apartments just when he felt inclined, but Lady Rochford could, and did. She also had the advantage of being well acquainted with her new mistress from their days of serving together in the chamber of Queen Anne, and of getting on with her. As Jane knew very well the new queen's morals were impeccable, which was one of the reasons why Henry loved her, and knew also that she was 'of no great wit'.[35] Her Privy Chamber would be calmer than that of Anne, but less exciting. She was a few years younger than Jane, and of no great beauty, so that serving her would be less demanding, and it might well be that Lady Rochford would be able to earn the Lord Privy Seal's goodwill at no very great cost to herself. There simply was not a lot to report – or at least not a lot in which Cromwell would be interested. One of Jane's early actions in the service of the new queen was to cultivate the friendship of the Princess Mary (or Lady Mary as she is properly called by this time). Mary had rejoiced greatly at the fall of the Boleyns, expecting her troubles to be over, but the king had forced her submission as the price of rehabilitation, and that had opened the way for the ever-amiable queen to welcome her again to the court.[36] Meanwhile Lord Morley had anticipated his daughter, and had visited Mary at Hunsdon, establishing an amicable relationship which was to last for the next twenty years. Jane took advantage of this opening. Although she was a Boleyn, that affinity had totally disintegrated, and she needed all the friends that she could get. So she exchanged New Year gifts with Mary in 1537, and was welcomed into that courtly circle that the princess now inhabited.[37] That circle also included the Seymours, and Jane must have felt a divided loyalty as she made her reports to the Lord Privy Seal. She was now firmly back in favour, and was a woman in her own right, something which she could never have been if George had remained alive. However, that situation did not survive for very long. In the spring of 1537 Queen Jane was known to be pregnant, and Henry became fretful and anxious, cancelling his planned trip to the north in order to be on hand. All appeared to be well, and Jane retreated into the usual female seclusion at Hampton Court in September. On 10 October she went into labour, and her attendants were permanently on duty. After an easy pregnancy, the labour was long and difficult and desperate anxiety prevailed until on the 12th the child finally appeared. It was a prince, and the rejoicings were thunderous. He was christened Edward on the 15th with the greatest possible ceremony, and the queen sat in the ante-chapel to receive the congratulations of all and sundry.[38] However, all was not well with her. A few days later she contracted puerperal fever, and in spite of the efforts of her servants and physicians, on the 24th she died. Her obsequies were duly celebrated in November, and in these Jane played a full part; nevertheless, when they were over, she was left without a role unless or until the king remarried. Nor was it by any means certain that she would be remembered if and when a new Privy Chamber was assembled.

She was thrown on her own resources again, and fortunately was able to exploit her father-in-law's declining health to secure a new financial deal. The Countess of Wiltshire died in 1538, and Thomas decided to put his affairs in order. Not without a certain pressure from the king via Thomas Cromwell, he settled certain lands on Jane, including the manor of Blickling in Norfolk, and sundry other manors, bringing her annual income up to about £200.[39] The negotiations were long and difficult because the settlement was for her life only, and the question of their destiny thereafter also had to be resolved. Eventually she signed the agreement, which was then secured by an Act of Parliament, a sensible precaution in the circumstances, and one in which the assistance of Thomas Cromwell can again be discerned.[40] The Earl of Wiltshire died in March 1539, and Jane was left comfortably provided for. Not only did she have the lands of her settlement, she also had the 300 marks a year which was due to her after his demise, a total of about £430 a year, which was enough to maintain her status as a viscountess in the country, or at court if she was called back to that environment. Meanwhile Henry was nervous, and anxious for allies. The so-called 'Exeter conspiracy' of 1538 had alerted him to the fragile state of the succession, dependant as it was upon a single young life. The Poles and the Marquis of Exeter had been involved in correspondence with the king's arch-enemy and traitor, Cardinal Reginald, who had come north in 1537 for the purpose of inciting the emperor and the King of France to military action against the schismatic English. He had failed, and the correspondence scarcely amounted to evidence of treason; but it did prove the disaffection of his family, and that was sufficient for Cromwell to act.[41] Especially since both the Marquis and the Countess of Salisbury had remote claims to the throne, which could have become horribly relevant if Edward had died. Henry also needed allies, particularly after the Treaty of Toledo had ended the war between France and the Empire in February 1539. He first tried the Schmalkaldic League in the summer of 1539, but their price proved too high in terms of religious commitment, so he turned instead to the Catholic Duchy of Cleves.[42] This negotiation rapidly merged with his search for a new wife, to which his council had been urging him since shortly after Jane Seymour's death, and in October 1539 a new treaty was signed, committing both sides to a policy of friendship, and Henry to a marriage with the duke's sister Anne. By November a new household was being assembled for the prospective queen and someone, possibly Cromwell, remembered Viscountess Rochford and recalled her from her Blickling retreat. It is not known exactly when Jane joined the new Privy Chamber, but she would have found herself in familiar company; Anne Basset, Lady Lisle's daughter, Katherine Edgecombe, her recently widowed aunt, Isabel Baynton and the young Katherine Carey, her sister-in-law's daughter.[43] Together they awaited Anne's arrival, and took part in all the ceremonies of greeting and marriage which followed. How soon her ladies became aware that all was not well in her union with the king we do not know. Communication would not have been easy since as far as we know, none of her English attendants spoke German, but it was apparently Jane Rochford who observed that if the queen were as innocent as she seemed, it would be a long time before a Duke of York appeared. When that marriage came to an end in July 1540, and Anne's household was broken up, Jane could have retreated to Blickling again, and might have been wiser to do so. However, she was by this time the most experienced of all the ladies-in-waiting, and the king decided that she should be recruited to the service of his latest bride.[44] It was not Cromwell this time who performed that office, because he had fallen from power on 10 June, and awaited the attentions of the executioner. It may have been her old mentor, the Duke of Norfolk, but by whosoever means, Jane was recruited to the Privy Chamber of Catherine Howard, and soon became her chief confidante.

Jane was therefore an experienced and shrewd operator, and it is out of character for her to act as Catherine's bawd during the summer progress. However her close involvement is proved not only by the testimony of others involved, but also by her own confession. She did indeed work discreetly (and sometimes less discreetly) to facilitate the queen's assignations with her lover, and had a very shrewd idea of what was going on. However improbable it may seem, she was an active agent in Catherine's infidelities.[45] Why she took such risks is not known. It is unlikely to have been through mere salacious curiosity, and although it is possible that she fancied Culpepper herself, that is not apparent from any of the evidence. It seems rather that she was aware that the queen was a light-headed young woman, and that her activities needed some sort of control. She may also have been genuinely fond of Catherine, and sympathetic to her dilemma of being married to such an unsatisfactory husband. So she took control of her mistress's love life, and thereby compromised herself in a manner which her history would not suggest as likely. By the time that the court returned to London, she was in it up to the neck.

7
Adultery Detected

While the court was still at York, at some point in late September or early October 1541, Mary Hall, sometime bedfellow of Catherine's at Horsham, told her brother, John Lascelles, about the antics in the 'maids' chamber' at the dowager duchess's establishment.[1] Why she did this is not very clear, but presumably she shared her brother's reformed religion, and was distressed by the Howard ascendancy at court, which was generally held responsible for the Act of Six Articles, and for the persecution of protestants which had followed it. Lascelles was in no doubt about the value of her information, particularly that appertaining to Catherine's relationships with Henry Mannox and Francis Dereham, so he took his story to the Archbishop of Canterbury at some time in mid-October. Howard influence may have predominated about the king during his progress, but those ministers who had been left behind in London to manage affairs were not Howard clients, and may well have welcomed this tale of pre-nuptial infidelity. Lord Audley and the Earl of Hertford were quick to appreciate the value of the stories which a worried Cranmer laid before them, and agreed that the king must be informed.[2] This could be a risky business because they all knew that Henry's affections were 'marvellously set upon' his young wife, and no one wanted to be the bearer of bad tidings. However they also knew that Henry would take news from his archbishop which he would not take from anyone else, so the task was delegated to Cranmer. He had a few days to decide how to communicate his message while the king travelled south, and eventually decided to do it in writing. He went to Hampton Court when news of Henry's arrival reached him, and finding the king at mass, passed him the letter, urging him to read it carefully in private.[3] When the king had done so, his reaction was surprising. Instead of becoming angry, he was puzzled and not particularly worried. He had apparently absolute faith in his wife's integrity, and was mainly concerned to protect her from slanderous and malicious gossip. He ordered an enquiry, but otherwise remained in good spirits, and nothing was said to Catherine at this point.

The Earl of Southampton, the Lord Privy Seal, was recalled to London to examine John Lascelles, who stuck to his story. Southampton was then sent down to Sussex on the pretext of a hunting trip to interview Mary Hall, who confirmed what she had told her brother, with circumstantial details. Catherine, she alleged, was in the habit of stealing the duchess's keys when the chamber door was locked, and of admitting whom she chose.[4] The king was wrong; there was substance in these accusations, and Sir Thomas Wriothesley quietly rounded up Mannox and Dereham. The latter was arrested for alleged piracy in Ireland during the previous year, and no one (apart from his immediate family) noticed the incarceration of Catherine's former music teacher. Terrified by their imprisonment, and possibly threatened with torture, they both confessed. Mannox testified that when he had come to the old duchess's service 'about five years ago' he had been set to teach mistress Catherine Howard the virginals, and that they had fallen in love. The duchess had found them embracing, whereupon she had given Catherine 'two or three blows' and had ordered that they were never to be alone together in future.[5] He did not admit to sexual intercourse, and claimed that he had been replaced in the lady's affection by Francis Dereham. Put on the spot by Mannox, Dereham's confession was a great deal more damaging. He admitted having know her carnally many times 'in a naked bed', but pleaded a contract of marriage between them in justification of his actions.[6] Already armed with these confessions, the Privy Council was in session when Southampton returned with Mary Hall's confirmation, which now looked all the more damning in the light of Mannox's and Dereham's testimony. They summoned absent members to rejoin them, and embarked upon a crisis meeting. How was this news to be broken to the king? For the time being they need not have worried, because Henry remained incredulous, protected by the thick skin of his own egotism. Catherine was a jewel among women, and had loved him with a 'perfect love', or so he continued to believe. The most that he was prepared to do was to order her to keep to her chambers and await his pleasure.

He was, however, avoiding her company, and on the morning of 6 November he ordered his dinner to be served in a field beside the palace, on the pretext of a hunting trip. There he met, by arrangement with Lord Audley and the Duke of Norfolk. He was still at great pains to conceal the potential scandal, but there were issues which needed to be addressed.[7] After this meeting he was sufficiently worried to order the whole council into an emergency session at the Bishop of Winchester's residence in

Southwark, whither he took himself by river without returning to Hampton Court. There, in an all-night session, he was confronted by the evidence which Wriothseley had wrung from Mannox and Dereham. The truth about Catherine's past could no longer be avoided, and the king's incredulity suddenly collapsed. She had represented for him the image of a youth which he had himself lost, and of an innocence which more than made up for her lack of wit, and now he was forced to conclude that he had deluded himself. Inevitably he blamed her for the deception, and is alleged to have threatened to torture her to death before collapsing into embarrassing tears of self-pity.[8] The old, self-confident Henry was temporarily in total eclipse, which as one reporter later noted 'was strange in [one of] his courage'. He lamented his ill-luck in marriage, and attempted to blame his council for this latest misfortune. They must have known something, and should have warned him. The fact that it had been his own evident passion for Catherine which had deterred any voices of caution was conveniently forgotten. His case, as Chapuys observed, resembled that of a woman who has buried ten husbands, and lamented the last more than all the others put together because for the first time, she did not know where the next was coming from.[9] Henry came from that meeting an old man, no longer capable of catching a young girl's fancy. He ordered his councillors to continue their investigations, and did the only thing which he was still capable of doing – he went hunting, for the purpose of 'diverting his ill humour' as one observer noted. It did not work.

The following day, 7 November, Cranmer was sent again to Hampton Court to interrogate the queen, and to arrange for her confinement to her apartment. Her jewels were to be inventoried, but she was not to be deprived of her 'privy keys', which meant that she was free to move around within her quarters.[10] In his subsequent report to the king, the archbishop was careful to emphasise her penitence:

> It may please your Majesty to understand that at my repair unto the queen's grace, I found her in such a lamentation and heaviness as I never saw no creature, so that it would have pitied any man's heart in the world to have looked upon her…

She had been in such a 'frenzy' that he had beaten a retreat, and returned the following day. It had been his intention, he confessed, to start by emphasising her 'demerits', but on finding her still in a very fragile state of mind, he had commenced by telling her that the king was disposed to be merciful, because otherwise she might have been 'drawn into some dangerous ecstasy', and his words of hope come too late.[11] Eventually, between floods of tears and bouts of hysterics Cranmer heard the full story of those days (and nights) at Horsham and Lambeth. She maintained that there had never been an espousal with Dereham, but rather that he had forced his attentions upon her rather than 'of her free consent and will'. This was damaging to Dereham, but also to herself, because if there had been some sort of a contract of marriage, followed by consummation, the worst that she could be accused of would be bigamy. That was bad enough when the injured party was the king, but might nevertheless have been sufficient to save her life.[12] However, Francis Dereham had been a mere gentleman, and not therefore of the status to have married with a Howard, so in spite of the fact that they had called themselves husband and wife, and acted accordingly, her confession is likely to have been true. It was also apparently the case that as soon as Cranmer had departed, she began to excuse and 'temper' her actions, repeating that she had not consented to his advances. In fact in the course of these interviews, and the conversations which surrounded them, she had displayed considerable instability of mind; first denying her offences, then abjectly confessing them, and finally seeking excuses.[13] It is not surprising that the council found her confession unsatisfactory in spite of the archbishop's best efforts. Perhaps suspecting that this would be the case, Catherine wrote directly to the king, in effect throwing herself upon his mercy:

I your grace's most sorrowful subject and most vile wretch in the world, not worthy to make any recommendations unto your most excellent majesty, do only make my most humble submission and confession of my faults. And where no cause of mercy is given upon my part, yet of your most accustomed mercy extended unto all other men undeserved, most humbly on my hands and knees do desire one particle thereof to be extended unto me although of all other creatures most unworthy to be called your wife or subject. My sorrow I can by no writing express, nevertheless I trust your most benign nature will have some respect unto my youth, my ignorance, my frailness, my humble confession of my faults, and plain declaration of the same, referring me wholly unto your grace's pity and mercy. First at the flattering and fair persuasions of Mannox, being but a young girl, suffered him at sundry time to handle and touch the secret parts of my body which neither became me with honesty to permit nor him to require. Also Francis Dereham by many persuasions procured me to his vicious purpose and obtained first to lie upon my bed with his doublet and hose and after within the bed and finally he lay with me naked and used me in such sort as a man doth his wife many and sundry times, but how often I know not, and our company ended almost a year before the king's majesty was married to my Lady Anne of Cleves and continued not past one quarter of a year or little above. Now the whole truth being declared unto your majesty, I most humbly beseech the same to consider the subtle persuasions of young men and the ignorance and frailness of young women. I was so desirous to be taken unto your grace's favour, and so blinded with the desire of worldly glory that I could not, nor had grace, to consider how great a fault it was to conceal my former faults from your majesty, considering that I intended ever during my life to be faithful and true to your majesty after, and nevertheless the sorrow of mine offences was ever before mine eyes, considering the infinite goodness of your majesty towards me from time to time ever increasing and not diminishing. Now I refer the judgement of all mine offences with my life and death wholly unto your most benign and merciful grace to be considered by no justice of your majesty's laws, but only by your infinite goodness, pity, compassion and mercy without the which I acknowledge myself worthy of most extreme punishment.[14]

It is to be wondered who helped in the composition of this most correct and moving epistle, because it does not read like the work of an air-brained twenty-year-old. Perhaps Jane Rochford was behind it. She had certainly composed very effective letters to Thomas Cromwell in the past, but there is no evidence to support such view, or to involve anyone else. The letter was probably referred to the council, and would have been no help in solving their main problem at that juncture, because it made no reference to any pre-contract with Dereham. It seems that the king and his advisers were working on the idea that such an understanding would have invalidated the king's marriage and would have been ground for an annulment.[15] That at least was the Howard point of view, and was shared by the dowager duchess, who was expecting Catherine to be returned to her care after her marriage had been dissolved, which was a worrying prospect. Other more hostile councillors reluctantly conceded that such a pre-contract might 'serve for her defence', and that the queen could be expected to escape with her life. On 10 November it was being rumoured abroad 'that Dereham had actually been betrothed to the queen before her marriage, which is therefore invalid'.[16] The canon law in such a case was unclear, but the general assumption was that any understanding followed by carnal copulation constituted a marriage, and that such copulation, even without an agreement, could do the same. If that had been the case, then Catherine's denial of any contract would become irrelevant. With the law so unclear, a lot would depend upon what the king chose to believe, and he was thought at this stage to favour mercy. However, the folly of the queen's behaviour after her marriage had not so far been revealed. She had taken Catherine Tylney, another of her Horsham playmates into her service, and under interrogation Tylney revealed the fact that Dereham had resurfaced in the queen's Privy Chamber, a fact of which the council had hitherto been unaware.[17] Caught out by this new revelation, Dereham furiously denied that he had resumed sexual relations with her, because as he said, his place had been taken by Thomas Culpepper. On 12 November the council noted that further scandal was likely to be shortly revealed. The king, as Marillac wrote to Francis I on the 11th, had been in council for several days 'which he is not wont to do', but all that he could glean was that 'the lady shall be no longer queen', and that the trouble was all on her account.[18] The next stage of the saga was about to begin.

Meanwhile Catherine was to be removed to the dissolved former monastery of Syon. Her household at Hampton Court was closed down, and her jewels confiscated to the king's use. These signs were ominous enough, but she was still styled queen and was attended by four ladies-in-waiting. She was given the furniture for three chambers 'without any cloth of estate', and a suitable wardrobe.[19] On 13 November the Lord Chancellor was instructed to call the whole council together, and to inform them of her 'abominable demeanour', but without mentioning the pre-contract because the interrogators were by then on a fresh scent, and that was no longer relevant. Alerted by Dereham, they were now on the track of Thomas Culpepper. He seems to have been quite unaware of his danger, until he was suddenly arrested and taken to the Tower, his role in the summer progress having been gradually and painfully extracted from several of Catherine's servants. On the 11th Wriothesley first questioned the queen herself about the matter 'now coming forth concerning Culpepper', but her answers appear to have been evasive because the council ordered further enquiries as to her communications with him. She admitted calling him a 'sweet fool', and giving him a cap and a ring, but denied any carnal relationship.[20] Her version of the story placed the blame squarely on him, and represented Lady Rochford as the agent who had engineered the whole affair for unknown reasons of her own. According the Catherine, Jane had sworn herself to secrecy about these meetings, and warned the queen that if she disclosed the truth she would 'undo herself and others'.[21] Unfortunately, however, Jane was not the only person to have been privy to these assignations. Catherine Tylney, Margaret Morton, and other members of the queen's household had at least a fair suspicion of what was going on, and all were now rigorously interrogated. Catherine had already been questioned about life at Horsham, but now she was subjected to a series of detailed questions which suggest that her inquisitors already had a fair idea of the outline of events, although whether they had obtained this from Culpepper or from the queen herself is not clear. The latter had been questioned a second time by Cranmer and Wriothesley, probably on the 12th, but the record does not survive.[22]

Catherine Tylney's evidence was disappointing for the simple reason that she had never been given the chance to see who it was that the queen had been meeting at unseasonable hours at Lincoln. Nor did she know what messages had been conveyed between her and Jane Rochford, or how late the queen had stayed up. She and Margaret Morton had been sent off to bed before they had a chance to find out, and only Jane Rochford had stayed on watch, although she often seems to have dozed off before her mistress was finished for the night.[23] The key witness thus became Jane, and unlike the others she was arrested and taken to the Tower for questioning. By this time she was aware that she was in deep trouble, and her answers were a desperate attempt to exonerate herself. According to her version of events, Catherine and Culpepper had contrived the whole affair between them, and far from playing the bawd, she was merely an unwilling servant who did as she was bidden. She admitted keeping watch, but denied ever hearing what endearments were exchanged between the loving couple, because she had kept her distance, as became a discreet servant.[24] On the other hand, she believed that coitus had taken place, and there was no incentive for her to have said that if it had not been true, because it elevated the whole business from a misdemeanour into a crime, and inevitably opened her to the charge of being an accessory after the fact. Culpepper would not admit to anything more than talk. They had talked in the maidens' chamber at Lambeth, when she had taunted him with wanting to make love to her; they had talked at Lincoln through the small hours of the morning, when he had professed that he loved her 'above all creatures'; and they had talked at York, where she had returned his expressions of love. He even admitted his desire for her, but denied that it had ever taken effect.[25] According to his version, the villain of the piece was Jane Rochford, who had consistently egged him on and provided the opportunities for their meetings. That rings true, but gets us no nearer to finding out what her motivation might have been. Moreover talk was not innocent, because the Treasons Act of 1534 had extended the penalties to those who 'do maliciously wish, will, or desire by word or writing, or by craft imagine' the king's death or harm. Almost anything that a subject might say in criticism of the monarch was therefore open to construction as treason; the intent was sufficient and no overt act was required.[26] Catherine wriggled hard, blaming everyone other than herself, but her own words were against her, and they testified in abundance to her desire for a lover who was not Henry, and whom she could only legitimately have enjoyed if Henry had been dead. This could easily be construed as 'imagining the king's death'; indeed it would be hard to see it in any other light, and that was treason by the Act of 1534.[27]

On 1 December 1541 Culpepper and Dereham were arraigned at the Guildhall in London on charges of treason, to which they both initially pleaded not guilty. However, when the evidence was presented on the king's behalf, and perhaps realising the futility of prolonging the proceedings, they both changed their pleas and were duly sentenced. When the council was satisfied that they had had 'gotten as much of Dereham as might be had' the king ordered the executions to go ahead, due warning being given to the condemned men to prepare their souls for eternity. On 10 December the sentences were carried out; Culpepper, because of his superior social status, being accorded the privilege of beheading, although Dereham's pleas to be accorded the same privilege were rejected.[28] Their fate spelt doom for the Howard clan. Lord William, the queen's uncle, was arrested on the 9th, the dowager duchess on the 10th and her daughter Lady Bridgwater on the 13th. The Tower was so full of Howard clients that the lieutenant was constrained to ask the king for permission to use the royal apartments as overspill prisons. The dowager was in particular trouble for having broken open two of Dereham's chests which had been entrusted to her for safekeeping, in order, it was alleged, to destroy incriminating documents.[29] What difference such papers would have made now that Dereham had been condemned and executed is not apparent. The Duke of Norfolk abased himself, alleging that he wept tears at the thought of the king's suffering through this second betrayal by one of his nieces. He even claimed the credit for having betrayed his stepmother's action over Dereham's chests. He was not touched, but the fabric of family politics which he represented was destroyed overnight. On 22 December the whole tribe were convicted of misprision of treason for concealing the queen's offences, and duly sentenced to indefinite imprisonment and loss of goods. They were pardoned in the spring of 1542 and their property was returned, but their power was over, and their rivals secured the king's ear.[30] Only the duke, that perennial survivor, remained as Lord Treasurer, but his power was much reduced, and the leadership of the conservative party at court remained with the Bishop of Winchester.

Meanwhile the judgement on her accomplices left Catherine nowhere to go. Those erstwhile friends and family members who had not been swept into the net of royal justice, dissociated themselves from her. On 22 December it was proclaimed that she should no longer be styled queen but only the Lady Catherine Howard. Her residence at Syon became an undisguised imprisonment, and she had nothing to hope for except the royal pardon, which seemed increasingly unlikely as Henry's indignation showed no sign of abating.[31] Rather strangely, she seems, intermittently at least, to have been quite cheerful under this regime. She was described unflatteringly as being 'fatter and handsomer than ever' and as being more imperious and difficult to please than she ever was 'living with the king her husband'.[32] Perhaps she had received some misleading indications of the King's grace, or perhaps she was simply unable to grasp the peril in which she stood, and was living from day to day. The other women who had been dragged into the affair, with the exception of Jane Rochford, were pardoned for their involvement. Mary Lascelles being specifically singled out for royal forgiveness on the strength of the testimony which she had offered. Under the intense pressure of her imprisonment, shortly before Christmas, Jane appears to have gone mad, which is probably an overstatement of the fact that she was periodically hysterical and overwhelmed. She knew that Henry's commissioners were evaluating her property, and that her life hung by a thread, and despair broke the bound of reason. However it did not suit Henry that she should escape because of lunacy. She was unquestionably guilty, and might even have been laughing at him behind his back as her husband had laughed with his sister. It was a thought not to be borne, so he sent his doctors to her, and even allowed her out of the Tower into the custody of Lord Russell, whose wife Anne was an old acquaintance. Russell House was on the Strand, and once there in a comfortable environment, Jane soon recovered.[33] Henry's vengeance could wait until after Christmas, which he spent at Greenwich without either music or festivities. December was a bleak month.

The king decided to proceed against his ex-wife and her accomplice by Act of Attainder. His reason for doing this is not altogether clear, except that no defence was possible against such an Act, and it may be that he did not want to raise again the question of a pre-contract. The parliament opened on 16 January, and the king was present at the opening session to hear the Lord Chancellor sing his praises, and to receive the homage of both houses.[34] The meeting had been called, Audley went on, not just for the sake of proceeding against Catherine Howard but for the purpose of producing good law and sound justice. Five days later, on the 21st, a Bill of Attainder was introduced into the House of Lords. Not only did it set out the crimes of Catherine and Lady Rochford, it also confirmed the sentences already passed upon the dowager duchess and other members of the house of Howard.[35] There are signs that the lords were not altogether happy with this Bill, and it was committed to the Archbishop of Canterbury, the Duke of Suffolk, the Lord Privy Seal and the Bishop of Winchester. The Lord Chancellor argued that 'the queen was in no sense a mean and private person' but rather a public and illustrious one, and that consequently no whisper of injustice must be allowed to tarnish their proceedings.[36] The committee did visit Catherine at Syon, but apparently only to reassure her that she would be tried 'by equal laws' as she would have been in the court of the Earl Marshall. Indeed they may well have pointed out that her judges would be the same men, because the court was composed of peers. She was not given any special rights of defence. The lords were still not happy and on 30 January another committee was appointed, consisting of the archbishop, the Duke of Suffolk and the Lord Privy Seal to consult with the king about the most desirable course. They were apparently reassured, because on 6 February the Bill was read for a second time.[37] It may have been amended at that stage, because it went through a further second reading on the 7th, before being read a third time on the 8th, and committed to the Commons. There it seems to have encountered no problems, and was returned to the lords on the 11th. As a result of earlier consultations, it was agreed that the king need not give his assent in person; instead he would do so by 'letters patent under the Great Seal of England', in order to spare him the grief and pain of hearing yet again the 'wicked facts' of the case.[38] It was an unusual statute in a number of ways, and it was not enrolled on the Chancery Roll as was normal with Acts of Parliament. In the first place it set out the treasons committed by the queen and Lady Rochford, and then confirmed the verdicts already passed on Culpepper and Dereham, and the misprision sentences passed upon the Howards. It also, however, included a clause authorising the assent by letters patent, and then went on to declare that any woman committing such an offence in the future would be similarly guilty of high treason.[39] This last was altogether extraordinary, because it laid down that if the king were to take a fancy to any young woman esteeming her 'a pure and clean maid' and to marry her on that assumption, if it turned out otherwise and she had concealed the fact, then she would be *ipso facto* guilty without further trial. As has been pointed out, that was as sure a way as any to make sure that in future the king would marry only widows![40]

Catherine may have received two visits from the lords while she was still at Syon; the first was designed to reassure her, as we have seen, and the second to hear any defence which she may have been able to offer. She, however, no longer saw any point in making excuses, and 'openly confessed and acknowledged' the great crime of which she had been guilty 'against the most high God and a kind prince'. She begged them to persuade the king not to attribute her offences to her entire family, and to bestow her clothes upon those maids who had been with her during the time of her marriage, because she now had nothing 'to recompense them as they deserved'.[41] The lords brought back the tidings that there were no longer any reasons not to complete the Act of Attainder, and that the former queen was facing death in a manner appropriate to her lineage. On 10 February, the day before her attainder received the royal assent, Catherine was taken to the Tower by river, and her remaining household at Syon broken up. Apparently she made some show of resistance, and had to be forcibly placed in the barge, which was discreetly covered to prevent the attentions of prying eyes. She was escorted on this last journey by two other boats, one bearing the Lord Privy Seal and members of the council, and other the Duke of Suffolk with an armed escort. The escort was unnecessary, because no one was going to intervene in this essentially ritual procession, as it went downstream to the traitors' gate. There, rather improbably, she was received with full royal honours before being escorted to her prison cell.[42] The unhappy Jane Rochford had been brought back to the Tower the day before, to be received with a kindness and consideration that did not mitigate the starkness of her plight. On 12 February the two women were warned for death the following morning. Their state of mind can be imagined.

8

The End of Catherine

The condemned women did not have long to wait. On 12 February they were warned for death the following morning, and had only hours to prepare themselves. As with all high-profile executions, this was to be a ritual in which they would be the star players, and it was imperative that they make a 'good end'. Consequently in addition to prayer, they had to give thought to what they would say, and what they would wear.[1] The Constable of the Tower, Sir John Gage, also had many preparations to make. The execution of a former queen was not an everyday event, and thought had to be given to how it was to be choreographed, and who would attend. Fortunately there was a precedent in the execution of Anne Boleyn nearly six years earlier. Sir Edmund Walsingham had been lieutenant of the Tower then too, so he knew what to do, and Anthony Anthony, who had kept a journal of those events, was still in post as a gunner, and could be consulted if necessary.[2] The same scaffold was brought out and re-erected on the green beside the White Tower. This was to be a 'private' execution, which only those invited would witness, and therefore was held within the precinct of the Tower. All those members of the council who were available would be expected to attend, and a select group of the citizens of London had been invited to observe the king's justice in action. The previous evening, Catherine had requested the block to be brought to her room, so that she could rehearse her last moments, and make sure that she positioned herself correctly. Now, in the cold light of a February dawn, it stood ready on its bed of straw, and the headsman was in attendance. The Duke of Suffolk was unwell, and the Duke of Norfolk absent on royal business, but the rest of the council had spent the night at Westminster in order to be on hand, and arrived by barge, just as the dawn was breaking. Chapuys noted that several lords and gentlemen who were not councillors also attended, but apart from the Earl of Surrey we do not know who they were.[3] Lord John Russell was present as a member of the council to witness the death of Jane Rochford who had so recently been his house guest, and must have found the whole event a considerable strain.

How the citizens were selected to attend we do not know, but presumably the livery companies were asked to choose representatives. As many of the aldermen as could be rounded up at short notice would have been there as well. Whether the Lord Mayor was present is not clear, but one man who was, was Otwell Johnson, the clothier and victualler whose customers had included many members of the queen's household. It is from his letter to his brother, written shortly afterwards, that we get our only eye-witness account of what transpired.[4] The Londoners apparently arrived on foot and entered the Tower by the western entrance, near to Petty Wales. Penetrating to the Inner Ward was quite an ordeal, since the visitors had to pass through three guarded gates before gaining admission to the north side of the

White Tower where the scaffold stood. Meanwhile Sir John Gage had welcomed his fellow councillors, and led them to their places in the stand which stood immediately behind the scaffold. The Londoners were to be the groundlings for the forthcoming show. We do not know how many of them there were, but it would have been far fewer than the thousand who had attended the execution of Queen Anne. By comparison, this was a genuinely private event.

The ladies were not to die together. Catherine, as became her former status, went first, and Sir John Gage led her out, warmly wrapped against the chilly morning air. She was accompanied by a group of four ladies who were to assist her in preparing for her ordeal. With their assistance she disrobed and ritually forgave her executioner for what he was about to do. Marillac says that she was so weak 'that she could hardly speak'. However, he was not there, and his report is at second hand.[5] Otwell Johnson, who was present, gives a very different impression, noting particularly her 'steadfast countenance' and courage. According to him she spoke briefly but clearly, acknowledging her faults and the justice of the sentence against her. She stated her belief in God's mercy and asked everyone to pray for the king. There were no recriminations, no protestations of innocence. It was a truly regal performance.

I saw the queen and the Lady of Rochford suffer within the Tower … whose souls [I doubt not] be with God, for they made the most Godly Christian end that ever was heard tell of [I think] since the worlds creation, uttering their lively faith in the blood of Christ only, with wonderful patience and constancy to the death, & with goodly words and steadfast countenance they desired all Christian people to take regard unto their worthy and just punishment with death for their offences against God heinously from their youth upward, in breaking of his commandments, and also against the King's Royal Majesty, very dangerously: wherefore they being justly condemned [as they said] by the laws of the realm & parliament to die, required the people [I say] to take example of them, for the amendment of their ungodly lives, & gladly to obey the king in all things, for whose preservation they did heartily pray, and willed all the people so to do, commending their souls to God, & earnestly calling for mercy upon him; whom I beseech to give us grace with such faith, hope and charity at our departing out of this miserable world to come to the fruition of his Godhead in joy everlasting.[6]

She who had once warned Thomas Culpepper not to admit to their liaison even in the confessional lest the king, who was supreme head of the church, might in some mysterious fashion find out about it, took her leave of the world as an orthodox Christian. She knelt in prayer and was then blindfolded before positioning herself carefully as she had rehearsed. The executioner took her head off with a single blow, raising it by the hair as ritual demanded. Her head was then wrapped in a white cloth and given into the care of her ladies, while her body was discreetly covered and taken to the nearby chapel of St Peter ad Vincula. The blood soaked straw was then removed and the scaffold washed in preparation for the second victim.[7]

Sir John Gage returned to the royal apartments, which served as a makeshift prison, and led out Jane Rochford. Jane had not witnessed Catherine's death, although she had probably heard the sound of it. She found herself confronted with a sea of familiar faces, men with whom in happier times she had laughed and danced, but who now sat stonily to see what she would do. She pardoned the executioner, as she was expected to do, and addressed herself to the last task of speaking to the world. According to Marillac she gave a long and rambling discourse, but that probably tells us more about his informant than it does about Jane. There is no verbatim transcript of her final speech, but Otwell Johnson, as we have seen, tells a very different story. She began by declaring her complete faith and trust in God, and went on to confess that she had committed many sins 'from her youth upward' and that she had offended the king's majesty very dangerously. She was therefore justly condemned by the laws of the realm and by the parliament. Let all those who witnessed her death take warning by it, and obey the king gladly 'for he is a just and Godly Prince'. She prayed for the preservation of the king, urged all those present to do the same and entrusted her soul to God. Of her recent hysteria there was no sign.[8] Her cloak was then removed and her eyes bandaged. The executioner then took her head off with a single blow, and her body joined that of her mistress in the chapel of St Peter. It was by then past ten o'clock, and the citizens and courtiers returned to the other business of the day. The king would be back from Waltham Abbey within a matter of hours, and would expect his council to be awaiting him. Although he was reported to be jubilant after his queen's execution, within a couple of months the ambassadors were reporting that the experience had aged him, and that he was often melancholy, 'sad and pensive' as Chapuys put it.[9]

There was also a fair amount of clearing up to be done. As early as December 1541 there were reports that Henry would take back Anne of Cleves, a hope which she seems briefly to have shared herself. There was even a rumour that she had borne Henry a child, an improbable story that even Marillac, who was not close to the court, reported sceptically.[10] The king never had the slightest intention of a reconciliation with his 'good sister', but it took several weeks for the reports to go away. For the time being, and in spite of the urgings of his council, Henry was in no mood for matrimony. He was coming to terms with the fact that he could no longer satisfy a young bride, and it was the realisation that his fires were spent which had caused the years to catch up with him. He was only fifty-one, but his self-indulgent lifestyle had wrought havoc with his body. He was fat and impotent, and his ulcerated legs were giving him constant pain. At the Tower there was routine tidying up required; the scaffold had to be cleaned and packed away, the executioner paid off and the guards returned to normal duties. The bodies of the victims had to be decently interred, although with minimal ceremony, and the heads reunited, because it would have been considered indecent to display them alongside Dereham and Culpepper on London Bridge. There was also the fate of the imprisoned members of the Howard affinity to be considered. Thirteen of them had been in custody since early December, when their goods had been inventoried and placed in the care of trusted officials. They included Agnes, Dowager Duchess, her son Lord William Howard, her daughter Katherine, Countess of Bridgewater, and Lord William's wife Margaret.[11] They had all been declared guilty of misprision of treason by the Act of Attainder which had condemned Catherine and Jane, and should in theory have remained in prison indefinitely. However the only one who had been seriously guilty of an offence had been Agnes, and there was something incongruous about keeping the stepmother of your Lord Treasurer in prison. Lord William also was a valued royal servant, so eight of the thirteen were pardoned during February, and on 25 March Chapuys reported that the rest of them would be freed shortly.[12] Their goods were restored to them, but no doubt the experience had given them a bad fright, and their ascendancy in the battle for influence at court was brought to an end, opening the way for a revival of that Evangelical influence which had ostensibly been vanquished with Thomas Cromwell. At about the same time, in April 1542 Anne Herbert, who had been given the custody of Catherine's jewels, returned them to the jewel house and was given a quittance for them.[13] By the spring of 1542 all trace of the former queen and her misdemeanours had been erased from the court, but not from the memory of the king – or Lord Morley.

Henry Parker had sat impassively in the House of Lords while his daughter's misdeeds were recited in the various readings of the Act of Attainder. What he really thought about her we do not know, but he must have pitied her untimely end. She was thirty-seven or thirty-eight, and had never presented him with the grandchildren which he had every right to expect. Nor had they ever been particularly close. He had not ridden to her rescue the last time that she had been in trouble after George's death, and did not do so now. Instead he and his wife simply accepted their loss as being one of the inevitable hazards of a life spent at court, which had been Jane's free choice. He did, however, retreat to his library and worked on a partial translation of Boccaccio's *De Claris Mulieribus*, which was a significant choice for a man who had just lost his daughter in distressing circumstances.[14] He worked hard, translating forty-six of Boccaccio's one hundred and four essays in time to present them to the king as a New

Year's gift in 1543, and his manuscript has been interpreted as a kind of epitaph for Jane. Ostensibly it was an acceptance of her guilt, because nearly all those in Morley's select translation were classical examples of female immorality, and designed to confirm Henry in his belief that he had been a victim of feminine passion and treachery. However, Julia Fox believes that it can be differently read. Looking at his account of Polyxena, the daughter of Hecuba and Priam, who was sacrificed to bring the Greeks fair winds for their homeward voyage, she notices that he inserted a complete phrase of his own into the text. 'O, that it was against all good order ... that so sweet a maiden should be devoured ... for to satisfy another woman's offence.' Clearly, she argues, the 'sweet maiden' was Jane and the 'other woman' was Catherine, for whose crime she was sacrificed. Polyxena had her throat cut, but Morley translates *iugulum* as neck rather than throat, which is another indication that he had Jane in mind.[15] It is possible (but by no means certain) that this was a scholar's testimony to his daughter's innocence, but if so, it must be admitted that it was very thoroughly coded. At the same time his wife, Alice, gave a peal of bells to St Giles Church, Great Hallingbury, near to their home, and while it was nowhere suggested that this was intended as a memorial to Lady Rochford, that might have been the private intention.[16] Her husband's sister, Mary Stafford, and her two children made not the smallest gesture of sympathy, but it may well be that Jane's parents remembered her with affection.

No one chose to remember Catherine with anything other than disdain. Her brilliant career had been snuffed out by her own ridiculous behaviour, leaving behind a family tainted with treason and a husband grown prematurely old. Her other legacy was a statute which declared it to be treason to marry the king unless the lady was a virgin; or rather it was treason for the lady to claim to be a virgin and not to be so in fact. Understandably candidates for the royal hand were in short supply among the ambitious young ladies of the court – the risks were simply too great.[17] Catherine had brought death or disgrace to everyone with whom she had been associated, and Henry would never forgive her. However, he would have grown old anyway, with or without her help, and her true legacy is political rather than personal. The king was of an age at which he might reasonably have sought peace with his neighbours, instead of which he plunged into new round of wars, and the conclusion is unavoidable. He was trying to recover that lost youth of which he felt that the wanton behaviour of an irresponsible damsel had deprived him. Why else would he have insisted on campaigning in person in France in 1544, when twenty years earlier he had been happy to leave the field command to the Duke of Suffolk? Suffolk was now an old man like himself, and yet the pair of them went off to Boulogne with the enthusiasm of a couple of schoolboys.[18] Henry had to squeeze himself into his latest suit of armour, which had been made to suit his generous proportions, and was hoisted onto his horse using a block and tackle. Neither his lieutenants nor his ally the emperor were keen on his participation, but he insisted. His honour, he argued, was at stake, especially since Charles had also announced his intention of taking part. His presence was decisive in a sense, because it was only after his arrival in the middle of July that it was decided to confine the campaign to Boulogne instead of advancing on Paris as the emperor wanted.[19] The king apparently enjoyed himself hugely, touring the siege works and personally placing some of the batteries. He was reported to be in better health and spirits than he had been for years. The siege commenced on 19 July, and on 11 September the castle was blown up. Three days later terms of capitulation were agreed, and on the 18th Henry entered in triumph.[20] It was all reminiscent of Tournai thirty years before, except that then the king had been in the prime of life, whereas now he was clinging to the wreckage. Orders were issued to the queen and council in England to despatch ships to Calais for his return journey, but in the event he stayed in Boulogne another ten days, supervising the building of new fortifications, and interesting himself in every detail. Meanwhile his ally the emperor, disgusted with his lack of co-operation in the campaign against Paris, had signed a separate peace with France at Crespy, leaving Henry to his own devices.[21] His reserves of energy now exhausted, the king returned to England on 30 September. He came back quietly, without any triumphal fuss, to face the bleak prospect of having to continue the war on his own, because Francis had no intention of giving up on Boulogne. The campaign came to a messy end when Norfolk and Suffolk abandoned Boulogne and retreated to Calais, an action for which they were lambasted by the king in personal letters which show no lack of commitment to the war. Fortunately the dauphin, in command of the French army, was unable to take advantage of this retreat, and the garrison at Boulogne was reinforced, but Henry seems to have drawn the conclusion that his armies would fall apart if he was not personally present to direct operations.[22] He was certainly present when Francis attempted his major counter-attack in July 1545. As the French fleet entered the Solent, the king was with his army ashore, awaiting the expected landing at Portsmouth. It never came, and daunted by the deployment of the English fleet the French retreated. This was the occasion on which the king witnessed the sinking of the *Mary Rose*, an event which caused him considerable distress. She had been launched in 1510, and another link with his youth was no more.[23]

This was to be Henry's last appearance in the field. Both sides had run out of money, and the following year he came to terms with the equally exhausted Francis, and signed the peace treaty of Camp. By the terms of this treaty, Boulogne was to remain in English hands for a period years, after which France could buy it back, if it could raise the money! So honour was, in a sense, satisfied on both sides and the warlike Henry could finally be laid to rest.[24] Politically he showed no signs of declining energy in the last months of his life, but physically he was a wreck who could move only with difficulty, and had to be carried any distance in a sedan chair. He eventually succumbed to his various ailments at the end of January 1547, leaving his realm to his nine-year-old son Edward. Catherine Howard had been only one factor in his decline, but she was a critical one. After his experience with Anne of Cleves, and in spite of the excuses which he offered, Henry was in need of reassurance that his sexual potency was unimpaired. This Catherine had appeared to offer, and had played the biddable maiden for his benefit. His libido had appeared to recover dramatically, and no one suspected anything wrong, except that she did not become pregnant. In view of the importance of children, both to the king and to the realm, this rules out any contraceptive activity on her part, and leads us to the suspicion that the union was never in fact consummated. Henry's considerable experience in such matters, and his continued satisfaction with his marriage argues against this, but we cannot be sure. When he had been unable to consummate his union with Anne, the king had made no secret of the fact, and if he had had similar difficulties with Catherine, he would surely have confessed it. In November 1541, when he was considering annulling his marriage on the grounds of pre-contract, he received a medical report which stated that his wife was barren, and although that was not followed up, it seems a likely explanation.[25] Whether he was actually impotent or not, it was clearly Henry's unsatisfactory performance as a lover which drove Catherine into adultery. She was sexually experienced and knew what it was like to have a young and able mate, so in spite of Culpepper's denials, it is likely that he slept with her during that progress to the north, and that Jane Rochford's suspicions were justified. Henry certainly thought so, and his rage as the cuckolded husband was based on that conviction. Thomas Culpepper had been a favoured member of the Privy Chamber, and the king felt doubly betrayed, because he had been in a sense responsible for bringing the two together, although it is extremely unlikely that he knew of the reported relationship between them before he married her. Catherine's big mistake was her failure to realise that there was a difference between being a young girl in the duchess's household and being the Queen of England. She should, of course, have made a clean breast of her earlier affairs when the king first showed a serious interest in her, although whether that would have deterred him we do not know. She was executed for adultery, which in a queen cast doubt upon the legitimacy of the royal offspring. The fact that there were no such offspring should have been relevant, but Henry was so enraged by her betrayal that it did not really matter. Her behaviour was stupid and childish, and probably more worthy of the penitentiary than the block, but the king willed otherwise.

Jane Rochford's behaviour was, if anything, more irresponsible, because she was older and more experienced in the ways of the court.[26] Whether she was an active pander or not we do not know, but what is certain is that she did nothing to try and deter Catherine from the disastrous course upon which she had embarked. By refusing her co-operation she could have nipped the Culpepper affair in the bud; instead of which she seems to have done all in her power to promote it. Her motivation for doing so is equally opaque, and the later supposition that she was mere licentious bawd will not do. There is no contemporary suggestion that she had a lover of her own, or was moved by a sense of common purpose. That she liked Culpepper is very likely, but that should have made her more willing to warn him of the dangers of the course on which he was embarking. It may simply have been that she took a vicarious pleasure in watching her young mistress enjoying herself, but there is plenty of evidence that she knew how dangerous it was, and she was executed eventually for being an accessory before the fact. By modern standards of justice, they were both falsely accused, but by the terms of the 1534 Act they were both guilty of imagining the king's harm.[27] They had offended the king in an area where he was particularly sensitive, and that in 1542 was sufficient to merit the death penalty.

9
Epilogue

No matter how besotted Henry was with Catherine, nor how disillusioned by her behaviour, the government of the country still had to be carried on, and issues of foreign policy addressed. As we have seen, the fall of Thomas Cromwell was followed by a period of Howard ascendancy at court, but this was not at all the same thing as a triumph for the conservative religious party. The king continued to steer his own idiosyncratic course, and to take evangelical initiatives from time to time. Only six persons were executed for breaching the Act of Six Articles, whereas 500 others, who had been rounded up, were pardoned for all 'heresies, treasons, felonies and other offences' committed before 1 July 1540.[1] Melanchthon might lament that the enemies of the gospel had triumphed in England, but Bucer reported that although Henry disagreed with the reformers on many points, he continued to be their friend. Latimer and Shaxton had resigned their sees, and the Evangelical party was in disarray, but the Six Articles were by no means the disaster which had been forecast. Of the 200 charged in London diocese with flouting its provisions, only three were eventually imprisoned, and in July

1541 a royal proclamation abolished many of the 'superstitious and childish' observances which had marked the feasts of St Nicholas and Holy Innocents.[2] In October a further proclamation repeated the instruction that all shrines were to be demolished, and ordered that lighted candles were to placed only before the rood. Neither of these were designed to lighten the heart of the Bishop of Winchester. Above all, and in spite of all efforts to remove him, Archbishop Cranmer stood firm in the royal favour, and was rescued from the so-called 'prebendaries plot' of 1543 by Henry's personal intervention.[3] Nor was Henry's distinctive churchmanship derailed by the fall of the Howards in the winter of 1541–2. The *King's Book* of 1543 was a conservative revision of the *Bishops' Book* of 1537, and it was not until the second and final fall of the Howards in 1546 that the Evangelical party could be said to have emerged as victorious from the battle for influence over the king's mind.

From about the time of his illness in March 1541, Henry was also angling for a closer friendship with the emperor. This had originally been Cromwell's policy, following the death of Queen Catherine in January 1536, and had been pressed upon him further by the friends and supporters of his third queen, Jane Seymour. In the midst of his preoccupation with his wife's infidelities, towards the end of 1541, he returned to the same theme, and took the matter up with Eustace Chapuys.[4] By the time that this happened, the king was clearly anxious to work off his ill-humour, and the effects of advancing age by having another go at the French, and realised perfectly well that he could only do that in alliance with Charles V. So he calculated on the breakdown of the Treaty of Toledo, and was justified in doing so when on 10 July 1542, hostilities were resumed between these inveterate foes. In June, just before the outbreak, but when it was clearly going to happen, he sent Thomas Thirlby, the Bishop of Westminster, to Charles with a proposal for a joint invasion of France in the summer of 1543. This proposal was welcomed by the emperor, and duly enshrined in a written agreement, into which both parties entered for reasons of their own.[5] The lack of any agreed strategy was only to emerge later in the day, when Henry eventually got around to honouring his obligations.

The reasons for this delay did not lie in any ailment, mental or physical, from which Henry might have been suffering, but in the situation with regards to Scotland. The king's strategy for dealing with James V was to attempt to induce him to follow his lead in dealing with the Church. However, James was heavily dependant upon ecclesiastical support, and was not to be tempted. As we have seen, his council successfully deterred him from visiting York in the summer of 1541, and raiding along the Scottish border increased as a consequence of Henry's ill humour. The Scots replied in kind, and each king wrote to the other, warning of the likely effects of such an escalation. There was no improvement in the situation, and in August 1542 Henry sent a force to the north commanded by the Duke of Norfolk in a threatening gesture which James could hardly have misinterpreted.[6] In September he increased the pressure still further, confronting the Scots commissioners who came to York in that month with a heavy list of demands relating to the discipline of the marches. He also repeated his invitation to James to visit England at Christmas, either to York or to London, in order to complete (as he put it) a treaty of amity. The Scots were complaisant, and agreed, he said, to all his conditions. They were not in a belligerent mood, but appear to have exceeded their instructions, and a period of dithering then followed as they awaited confirmation of the concessions which they had made. This did not come, and Henry's patience was short. He delivered an ultimatum; either the Scots agreed to release some English prisoners that they held, and gave pledges for James to come to England, or his army would march.[7] In October he ordered the Duke of Norfolk to make a raid in strength into the Scottish lowlands. Norfolk was hampered by a lack of carts and a shortage of victuals, and his enterprise lasted only six days, but it was immensely destructive. The king was gratified, and wrote congratulating the duke. He also ordered that a force of 5,000 men should remain in the border region to provide a defence against the expected Scottish counter attack, and Norfolk was to remain in command.[8] The purpose behind all this military bluster was to deter James from acting as his father had done when he had taken advantage of Henry's preoccupation with France to invade. That campaign had come to a bloody end at Flodden, but there was no guarantee that such a success would be repeated, and the king preferred to be safe than to be sorry. As such it was probably unnecessary because James was not prepared for war, and in any case had no intention of repeating his father's mistake. However, he could not afford to ignore the blatant provocation of Norfolk's raid, and after making a ritual appeal to Rome for aid, he launched about 20,000 men into the Debatable Lands, north of Carlisle. This force, as it transpired, lacked both experience and tactical know-how. On 24 November, while skirting the bogs of the Esk Valley, it was caught by a smaller but better organised English army under the command of Sir Thomas Wharton, Warden of the West March. Taken at a major tactical disadvantage, the Scots infantry broke and ran.[9] This was no bloodbath, nor a victory to be compared to Flodden, but the Battle of Solway Moss left a large number of Scottish peers and lairds in English hands, most of whom were quickly despatched to London.

Meanwhile fate, or providence, had dealt the King of England a strong hand. On 8 December 1542 Mary of Guise, Queen of Scots, was delivered of a daughter, and on the 14th James V died. He had not been present at Solway Moss, and the story that he died of sorrow at that defeat is a bit of constructive fiction. In fact he seems to have died of venereal disease contracted in one of his numerous amours, but that is not certain either; what is clear is that his death was unexpected. His only son having died in 1541, he was succeeded by his daughter, Mary, with a long minority ahead of her, and in the short term the Council of Scotland assumed the responsibility for government.[10] If Henry had invaded at that point, the council would have been unable to stop him, but that was no part of his plan. The major forces which he was gathering were located in the south and aimed against the French. He had been merely intending to prevent James from taking advantage of him, and that had now been achieved, although not in the way anticipated. However, the temptation to take advantage of the Scots' difficulties to re-assert his claim to suzerainty over the kingdom was too strong to be resisted. So he came up with a plan to marry the infant queen to his own son, Edward, then aged about five. If both children lived this would ensure the future union of the crowns, and in the meantime give Henry a controlling say in the government of Scotland.[11] The fact that he had numerous Scottish prisoners in his hands strengthened his position still further, and before they were released in January 1543 they were compelled to swear an oath to uphold the English position in Scotland, thus forming (it was hoped) the nucleus of an English party. Meanwhile, things were not going according to plan, because on 3 January the Earl of Arran was proclaimed Governor of Scotland during the minority of the queen, with a right of succession if Mary should die.[12] This action was taken by the council without consulting him – a very practical way of refuting his claim to overlordship. However, Henry did not attempt to intervene, except through the prisoners, who were by then at Berwick on their way home, and whose role was now likely to be more difficult than any of them had anticipated. In view of his earlier attitude, Henry's lack of belligerence in this situation is surprising, because he was undoubtedly in control of policy. It may be that he was again feeling his age, but more likely because reports had reached him that Arran was a 'favourer of the Gospel' and no friend to the kirkmen. Indeed, he arranged the arrest of Cardinal Beaton, and had written to Henry not only about the possibility of reforming the kirk, but also of negotiating a treaty of peace and marriage between the kingdoms.[13] In other words, he seemed surprisingly conformable to the king's purposes, and on 20 February Henry offered him a three-month truce to enable these negotiations to take place, and this was accepted by Arran, in the name of Mary, Queen of Scots. Nevertheless the weeks were slipping by, and Henry was reluctant to honour his commitment against France while Scotland was in any sense unfinished business. So in mid-March he sent Ralph Sadler to the north with instructions to report on the situation there, and bearing a letter to Arran from the king instructing him how to carry out a reformation. The letter produced assurances of the earl's anti-papalism, which were downright dishonest in the circumstances, and no action whatsoever was taken. Sadler reported that there were three parties in Scottish politics: the governor and his supporters, who looked to England; the clergy and their allies who looked to France; and a neutral party who looked only to their own interests and would join with whichever of the others emerged on top.[14] However, he was wrong, because the governor was also playing for his own hand and feeding the English king with false information to prevent him from intervening. In fact he released Cardinal Beaton from confinement and secretly placed the kingdom under papal protection. This was not worth a great deal, but was a significant gesture towards the pro-French party, in support of which the Earl of Lennox had come from France with gold, and with an envoy promising French aid if the English should invade. In other words the politics of Scotland were more complex, and less favourable to the English, than Sadler believed.[15]

In June Arran was still fending Henry off with a show of compliance. He sent commissioners to London to negotiate a treaty, and this was duly completed at Greenwich on 1 July. By its terms Mary was to be married to Edward, but was not to come to England until she was ten years old. For some unknown reason the king interpreted this limited success as evidence that the government of Scotland had now submitted to him, and that he was free to proceed against France.[16] He had renewed his treaty with the emperor in February, and although this was kept secret until May, by 22 June Henry was prepared to proceed to hostilities. He gave the French ambassador an ultimatum which was bound to be rejected, and shortly after sent about 5,000 troops to aid in the defence of the Low Countries, and on 6 June there was an engagement between the two navies in the Narrow Seas. It looked as though all-out war was about to commence. However, events in Scotland again supervened. Civil war was threatening in that kingdom as Lennox and Beaton rose in rebellion against the governor, and Henry was forced to prepare 5,000 men to go to Arran's assistance. On 31 August they were put on standby, as it appeared that the earl was fighting for his political life. They were not needed, however, as on 5 September came the crushing tidings that Arran had changed sides and joined the cardinal at Stirling.[17] The English party was not quite destroyed, but its leadership now devolved on the Earl of Angus, who was not up to the job, either in terms of character or resources. Henry wanted to send an army to his support, but was deterred by the fluidity and complexity of Scottish politics, which might have landed such a force in a hostile land without allies. So for the time being he confined himself to issuing unrealistic instructions to Angus, who did not have the means to fulfil them, even if he had had the will. Not knowing what else to do, Henry blustered. The Scots must abandon France and honour the treaties between the two countries, which he considered almost annihilated by their failure to implement them. He threatened war and authorised the seizure of some Scottish ships, but went no further, expecting the Earl of Angus to do his work for him, which he showed no sign of doing. On 11 December the Scottish parliament annulled the Treaty of Greenwich, and on the 15th renewed all the old treaties with France.[18] Twelve months on from Solway Moss, and all Henry had achieved in Scotland was a country united against him, and an Auld Alliance fully refurbished. His own clumsiness and lack of understanding were largely to blame for this situation, and that can partly be attributed to his physical deterioration. He had become more tyrannical with advancing years, and less willing to accept cautious advice. He was also unwilling to recognise his own limitations, imagining that he had servants and agents, whereas in fact he had only opportunistic allies who were playing for their own hands. Both Arran and Angus come into that category. That same false confidence which had led him to trust Catherine so implicitly led him to trust the Scottish earls, with the result that he felt the same sense of betrayal when his expectations were disappointed. That same violence of passion which had caused him to call for a sword to kill the ungrateful girl now prompted him to order two violent raids on the lands of Angus and his supporters. He was sorely missing the political skills of Thomas Cromwell, and when the black mood was on him, he acknowledged the fact, lamenting his own precipitate action.

However, just as he had not killed Catherine with his own hands, so he held back from attacking the lands of the Earl of Angus. The latter succeeded in persuading him that he had not been guilty of betrayal, and still in fact supported the English cause.[19] The main English army was stood down until the spring of 1544, when it would be deployed elsewhere. Meanwhile the Earl of Lennox, who had arrived from France in the spring of 1543, had come over to the English side, giving it an additional shred of credibility. On the strength of this, by March 1544 Henry was full of grandiose plans. He would work through Lennox and Angus to secure control of Scottish affairs; he would have the word of God preached throughout the land; and secure the person of Queen Mary until the time came for her delivery to Prince Edward. He would be named as her protector during her infancy, and would send an army which would set them up as a government, with Lennox as governor. With the aid of the English party he would make sure that Scotland would never again assist France, or trouble England.[20] Alas for all such plans!

It quickly became apparent that Lennox could not fulfil his side of this audacious bargain, and the king quickly reverted to a policy of direct action. This was originally entrusted to the Duke of Suffolk, but by March the king had decided that Suffolk would be needed for his main expedition against France, and what was essentially a sideshow against Scotland would be commanded by the Earl of Hertford with the Lord Admiral, Viscount Lisle, in control of the fleet. On Hertford's advice this was to be a quick in-and-out raid, not designed to subdue the Scots, but to deter them from intervening on the French side in the forthcoming war. A small force of about 4,000 men would go in overland on the traditional route north from Berwick, while the main army, some 15,000 strong, would attack Edinburgh direct from the sea.[21] There were difficulties in assembling enough ships for such an operation, and then the weather was bad, but on 2 May they landed at Leith, and put to flight a much smaller Scottish force under the command of Cardinal Beaton which endeavoured to impede their progress. The cardinal was apparently the first to run away, which caused the English much mirth. Having plundered the town (and found it surprisingly wealthy) Hertford then proceeded to Edinburgh, and after blowing in the gates, set the place on fire in accordance with his instructions. He did not attempt to take the castle, the guns of which inflicted a number of casualties on his troops, but English horsemen raided as far as the gates of Stirling, plundering as they went. On 15 May the English retreated, not having had to fight a serious engagement.[22] So great was the plunder, including guns, that the ships were fully loaded and the troops went back overland, meeting only notional resistance. The main consequence of this destruction was the discredit of Arran as governor, and his replacement by the queen mother, Mary of Guise, which meant that Henry was as far as ever from controlling the Scottish situation. Lennox remained loyal, but there was little that he could do, and the Scots in general were more bitter against the English than they had been before. It did not suit the queen mother to seek to intervene on the French side during the king's campaign in France, but that owed little to the intimidating effects of Hertford's activities.

By the time that Hertford left Scotland, the main 'army royal' was already assembling at Calais, and he was instructed to send 4,000 of his men direct to the rendezvous.[23] Henry's intention to campaign in person was strongly resisted, both by the emperor and by his own council, but for reasons which we have already noticed, he insisted. Attempts were made to dissuade Charles from campaigning in person, but these were unsuccessful, and as long as the emperor was in the field, Henry felt that he could not withdraw without loss of face – at least that was what he said. At the same time the strategy of the campaign was being debated. The king argued for local operations, bearing in mind the problems of supply and his need to safeguard the security of Calais, but the emperor was not to be persuaded, having set his heart upon an attack on Paris.[24] This debate was still ongoing while the army was assembling at Calais, and prompted the Duke of Norfolk to complain that he had no idea where he was supposed to be going. As we have seen, it was resolved in practice by Henry deciding to attack Boulogne, and effectively to abandon the plan for a joint attack on the French capital, a position which he was still defending to Imperial representatives as late as the end of July. Charles had no option but to accept his decision, but he did so with a bad grace and, taking advantage of the feelers which Francis was putting out, signed a separate peace with France on the same day that Henry entered Boulogne, 18 September. If the king of England wanted a piece of France, and insisted on campaigning on his own terms, then he could do so without an ally. With Charles's withdrawal from the war, most of the German horses serving with the Duke of Norfolk at the siege of Montrueil withdrew as well, leaving the duke in considerable danger. He extricated himself with difficulty, and Henry now had another betrayal to add to his catalogue of grievances.[25] First Catherine, then the Scots and now the emperor; by the end of 1544 he was feeling seriously ill used, and that occasioned the black mood from which he was suffering at the New Year of 1545. The fact that each of these betrayals had been brought on by his own actions never seems to have occurred to him.

Meanwhile the king had married again, not this time in a spirit of lascivious speculation but in the course of duty, urged on by his council. On 12 July 1543 he wedded Catherine, the widow of John Neville, Lord Latimer, who was thirty-one years old and had already been married twice before. Catherine was the daughter of Sir Thomas Parr of Kendal in Westmorland, a well-established courtier who had died in 1517, leaving three young children. His widow, Maude, had never remarried and Catherine had been brought up on her modest estate in Northamptonshire. She received the conventional education of an aristocratic girl, but her mother retained contacts with the court, and in 1529 secured a marriage for her with Edward Borough, the son of Thomas, Lord Borough.[26] This had been a good marriage, but Edward was in poor health, and had died in 1532, leaving his twenty-year-old widow childless. It is by no means certain that the union was ever consummated. By that time Maude had also died, but the Parr family rallied round, and secured in

1533 a marriage for Catherine with John, Lord Latimer, a forty-year-old widower with grown children. John Neville had been involved in the Pilgrimage of Grace. He escaped any penalty, but the experience broke his health, and for the second time Catherine found herself wedded to an invalid. However, for that reason he moved his residence to Charterhouse Yard in London, and that restored Catherine's links with the court, where she became friendly with Princess Mary. It is thought to have been through this friendship that she first encountered Henry, some time before the end of 1542.[27] It was probably also through contact with the king's well-educated daughter that her own intellectual curiosity was aroused, and she began to learn Latin. Unlike Mary, however, education appears to have moved her into the evangelical camp, and her interest in the bible and the Continental reformers developed before she met Henry. When Lord Latimer died in March 1543, Catherine was being actively pursued by Sir Thomas Seymour, the younger brother of the Earl of Hertford, who was the political leader of the Evangelical party at court. Sir Thomas's religious sympathies are not known, but were probably similar to his brother's. Seymour was swept aside by the king. Henry's first gift to her is dated 16 February, while Lord Latimer was still alive, and when he died on 2 March, her conspicuous presence in the court was noted by shrewd observers.[28] What attracted him to her is not known, but it was not sexual desire of the kind which he had lavished on Catherine Howard. His fires were spent and he knew it. Nor was it her brilliant wit, because Catherine was a dutiful thinker rather than a spontaneous one, and never famous for her repartee. It seems that what Henry was seeking was a comfortable companion for his declining years, and saw that in this dignified and agreeable lady. Although his last Succession Act of 1544 dutifully provided for any offspring born between the king and his present queen, that was not a realistic expectation.[29]

Catherine, however, achieved a number of things as queen. In the first place she brought all three of the king's surviving children into the royal household. She was friendly with Mary, who was twenty-seven, and a loving stepmother to Elizabeth, aged ten, and Edward, aged six. Although it was the king who appointed tutors for the latter, her influence has rightly been detected in the nomination of Sir Anthony Cooke, John Cheke and William Grindal, all noted humanists, to these positions. Her patronage of the humanists was one of the fruits of her belated education, and one of the most profitable.[30] She also encouraged Mary to translate part of Erasmus's *Paraphrases* on the New Testament, and Elizabeth to do the same with Margaret of Navarre's *Mirror of a Sinful Soul*. Her own Evangelical priorities were well reflected in her *Prayers Stirring the Mind unto Heavenly Meditations*, although that carefully steered clear of the Protestantism which only became obvious after Henry's death had made it safe to appear.[31] In spite of that, she took risks, becoming noted in reforming circles as 'Godly' because of her habit of holding scripture classes with her ladies-in-waiting, and listening to regular sermons by her chaplains – not activities for which Catherine Howard had been remarkable. She also discussed religion with the king, a thing which nobody else apart from Archbishop Cranmer dared to do, urging him apparently to complete his reformation of the Church by cleansing and purging it of 'popish dregs'. This activity eventually landed her, according to John Foxe, in serious trouble.[32] As his ailments troubled him more, he sent for her less often, these discussions became intermittent, and after one such session he remarked

...a good hearing it is when women become such clerks; and a thing much to my comfort to come in mine old days to be taught by my wife...

The Bishop of Winchester, who had overheard this observation, took it as a golden opportunity to squash this dangerous woman, who had so severely undermined his influence, and having agreed with the king on the unseemliness of such activities, offered to prove to Henry the treasonous heresy which he was 'nursing in his bosom'.[33] The plan was to charge her sister and two of her Privy Chamber first, then to search their rooms and on the strength of the evidence uncovered to whisk the queen off to the Tower – a plan to which Henry apparently agreed. Articles were drawn up to that effect, and the members of the Privy Chamber sworn to secrecy. A strange thing then befell, because a copy of the articles was accidentally dropped by a member of the council and brought to the queen, who immediately perceived her danger. Going to the king, she threw herself on his mercy, professing that her interest in religion had only been for the purpose of learning from his inestimable wisdom. Gross though this flattery may have been, Henry had responded to it, replying, 'And is it even so sweetheart, and tended your argument to no worse end? Then perfect friends are we again as ever at any time heretofore.' The following day, when the Lord Chancellor arrived with an armed escort to escort the queen and her ladies to prison, he found them walking with the king in the palace gardens and was sent away having been called a fool and an arrant knave for his pains.[34]

It is hard to know what to make of this story. Was the king really so suggestible that he could be turned from a considered purpose by a word of humble submission? Or was he only pretending to be convinced by Gardiner's arguments? If Foxe's narrative is authentic – and there is no corroborative evidence – it leaves us with a mystery surrounding the king's behaviour. Other contemporary evidence suggests that even in the last months of his life, Henry was very much in control, so it is not to be ascribed to any senile deterioration.[35] On the other hand, it is consistent with other dramatic changes which had occurred in the past; with his sudden turning against Anne Boleyn and Thomas Cromwell for example, when there was no question of there being anything amiss with him. He enjoyed playing games with his council, inducing them to take action which he could then repudiate. He had done this a couple of times with Thomas Cranmer, and it could be seen as demonstrating who was really in control. What is surprising is that he needed such reassurance. Our conclusion should probably be that for all his magnificent exterior, and awesome presence, Henry lacked self-confidence. He was prepared to abandon his first wife, but only on the grounds that his marriage had offended the laws of God; and he was prepared to take radical action against the Church, but only on the basis of old authentic laws. Henry never saw himself as an innovator, and was careful always to amend the laws before he took advantage of them – particularly the law of treason.[36] He needed continually to reaffirm his personal control, and his unique relationship with God; so he destroyed the Duke of Buckingham, Wolsey, Anne Boleyn, and Thomas Cromwell in turn, as much for daring to take him for granted as for anything which they had done. This lack of confidence extended to his sex life. After his first few years of marriage, he seems to have had difficulty getting any woman pregnant, and went through two or three mistresses (as well as his wife) before begetting Henry Fitzroy, who was to remain his only bastard. Anne Boleyn's alleged mockery of his intermittent impotence was one of the most damaging charges against her, because it touched the king on a uniquely sensitive spot. His failure with Anne of Cleves, although lavishly excused at her expense, revived all those fears in an acute form. Which was why his passion for Catherine Howard, so publicly demonstrated, was of such critical importance to him. The fact that he failed again had a devastating effect upon his ego. We do not know what happened between them, but the fact that she succumbed to the temptation of other beds tells its own story. Not only did she betray a personal trust but a public confidence. Henry took refuge in war and diplomacy to recover his public face, and did so successfully, but beneath the imposing surface, he was the old man which his fifth wife had helped to create. She was guilty of a subtle form of regicide.

Catherine's family survived the débâcle of her conviction, and of their own attainder for misprision. Her uncle the Duke of Norfolk was sufficiently high in the king's confidence to be entrusted with the command (under the king) of the expeditionary force to Boulogne in 1544, although he never fully recovered his influence in the council.[37] Her brothers, George, Henry, and Charles, dissociated themselves from her and escaped the net of the family attainder, while her cousin Henry, the Earl of Surrey, was not close enough to be involved. The final destruction of the Howards as a political force came in 1546, with the attainder of the Duke and the Earl of Surrey for conspiring to seize control of the minority government of Edward VI. Surrey was executed and the duke, reprieved by the king's own death at the end of January 1547, remained in prison throughout Edward VI's reign. He was restored to his offices and estates as an eighty-year-old on Mary's accession, and returned to the council, but died in the following year, to be succeeded in his title by his grandson, Thomas, who became the fourth duke.[38] This Elizabethan duke died for treason in 1572, having aspired to the hand of Mary, Queen of Scots, and the Howard influence was finally extinguished. By that time Catherine's brief career had long since been consigned to the makers of scandalous stories, in whose hands it has largely remained since – a dreadful warning to royal ladies who put gratification before the duties of their position.

Notes

Introduction: A King under God

1. Henry's hereditary claim ran through his mother, Margaret Beaufort, who was the granddaughter of John, Marquis of Somerset. John was in turn the son of John of Gaunt, by his third wife, Katherine Swynford, and thus a grandson of Edward III. Unfortunately Gaunt and Katherine had not been married at the time of his birth, so although their subsequent marriage legitimated him for most practical purposes, that did not necessarily extend to a claim to the throne.

2. S. B. Chrimes, *Henry VII* (1972), p.93.

3. Edward Hall, *Chronicle* (ed. 1806), p.503.

4. *Rotuli Pariamentorum*, VI, p.270; P. R. Cavill, *The English Parliaments of Henry VII* (2009), pp.29–33.

5. Ibid, p.241.

6. Garrett Mattingly, *Catherine of Aragon* (1963), pp.97–9.

7. J. J. Scarisbrick, *Henry VIII* (1968), pp.33–6; David Loades, *Henry VIII* (2011), pp.86–9.

8. *Oxford Dictionary of National Biography*.

9. Barbara Harris, *Edward Stafford, third Duke of Buckingham* (1986).

On Henry's relations with his aristocracy, see Helen Miller, *Henry VIII and the English Nobility* (1986).

10. Of the fifty peers who were alive when Henry died, thirty-four were of his own creation. Miller, *Henry VIII*, pp.259–263.

11. Peter Gwyn, *The King's Cardinal*, (1990) *passim*.

12. On the problems of security at the Tudor Court, see David Loades, *The Tudor Court* (1986), pp.85–95.

13. David Loades, *Mary Tudor: a Life* (1989), pp.14–15.

14. *Cal.Ven*, II, p.479; Scarisbrick, *Henry VIII*, p151.

15. Beverley Murphy, *Bastard Prince: Henry VIII's Lost Son* (2001), pp.36–8.

16. David Loades, *The Boleyns* (2011), pp.50–1.

17. E. W. Ives, *The Life and Death of Anne Boleyn* (2004), pp.325–7.

18. The degree to which Henry was supported by his people can be measured (very roughly) by the extent to which dissidents were denounced by their neighbours, see G. R. Elton, *Policy and Police* (1972), pp.327–382.

19. David Loades, *The Six Wives of Henry VIII* (2009). Henry's first two marriages had been taxing in different ways. Catherine had been obstinate in her refusal to accept rejection while Anne had had a lively political intelligence, and a sharp wit which she exercised at the king's expense.

20. *Original Letters Relative to the English Reformation*, ed. H. Robinson II, p.205; Retha Warnicke, *The Marrying of Anne of Cleves* (2000). J Strype, *Ecclesiastical Memorials* (1822), I, p.462.

21. G. R. Elton, *The Tudor Constitution* (1982), pp.242–3.

22. Ibid, pp.237–8.

23. For a recent study of Henry's doctrinal conservatism, see G. W. Bernard, *The King's Reformation* (2005). The king nevertheless opened the door to Protestantism by arranging for his son to be

tutored by men who were of that persuasion – a fact which he apparently declined to recognise.

24. Lacey Baldwin Smith, *A Tudor Tragedy* (1961), pp.185–6.

25. Elton, *The Tudor Constitution*, p.13.

26. 'An Homily on Obedience' in *Certain Sermons or Homilies appointed by the King's Majesty to be declared and read...* (1547).

27. Statutes 31 Henry VIII, c.14; 25 Henry VIII, c.22; 28 Henry VIII, c.7. Fisher and More had gone to the block (1535) and Barnes, Jerome and Garrett to the fire (1540).

1 The Much Married King

1. For a full discussion of this issue, which was to be of great importance in 1527–30, see Garrett Mattingly, *Catherine of Aragon* (1963), pp.48–9.

2. When Isabella died in 1504 her heir was not her husband but her daughter Juana, married to Philip of Burgundy. Ferdinand nevertheless tried to cling on to power, and Henry decided to side with Juana and Philip. The text of Prince Henry's declaration is printed in G. Burnet, *History of the Reformation* (ed. N. Pocock), IV, (1865), pp.17–18.

3. J. J. Scarisbrick, *Henry VIII*, pp.12–14; Edward Hall, *The Union of the two noble and illustre families....* (1548), f.ii.

4. *Letters and Papers...of the Reign of Henry VIII*, ed. J. S. Brewer *et al.* (1862–1910), I, no. 84.

5. Scarisbrick, pp.27–9.

6. David Loades, *Henry VIII*, p.56.

7. David Loades, *The Six Wives of Henry VIII*, pp.22–3.

8. Edward Hall, *Chronicle* (ed. 1806), p.507.

9. Wood, *Letters of Royal Ladies*, I, p.158; Scarisbrick, p.18.

10. Mattingly, *Catherine of Aragon*, p.108.

11. Hall, *Chronicle*, p.520.

12. David Loades, *Mary Tudor: a Life*, pp.14–5.

13. The only precedent in English history was the unsuccessful proclamation of Matilda in 1141. There was a closer example in the reign of Catherine's mother, Isabella of Castile, but that was not altogether encouraging.

14. P. Gwyn, *The King's Cardinal*, p.351; Beverley Murphy, *Bastard Prince* (2001), pp.28–9.

15. G. R. Elton, *The Tudor Constitution* (1982), p.200.

16. David Loades, *The Boleyns*, p.177. Henry Carey was born on 4 March 1526.

17. The standard way to legitimate a bastard was for the parents subsequently to marry, but that was out of the question in this case. The only alternative was via a special papal dispensation, but that could be challenged, and was not considered sufficiently secure.

18. Her messenger was a Spanish servant called Fernando Felipez, who travelled by sea to Spain to outwit Henry's intended interception. Scarisbrick, p.157.

19. For a full account of these comings and goings, see Henry A. Kelly, *The Matrimonial Trials of Henry VIII* (1976), pp.54–134.

20. P. Gwyn, *The King's Cardinal*, pp.549–99.

21. *Calendar of State Papers, Venetian*, IV, p.754; D. Wilkins, *Concilia* (1737), III, p.746.

22. In the so-called 'Collectanea Satis Copiosa', produced by his 'think tank' in 1530; Graham Nicholson, 'The Act of Appeals and the English Reformation' in *Law and Government under the Tudors*, ed. by J. Scarisbrick, C. Cross and D. Loades (1988), pp.31–51.

23. Scarisbrick, *Henry VIII*, pp.329–30.

24. R. J. Knecht, *Francis I* (1982), p.266.

25. D. MacCulloch, *Thomas Cranmer* (1996), pp.228–9.

26. Guy Bedouelle and Patrick Le Gal, *Le 'Divorce' du Roi Henry VIII* (1987), pp.47–198.

27. MacCulloch, *Thomas Cranmer*, pp.84–9.

28. G. R. Elton, *Thomas Cromwell* (1991), pp.8–11.

29. For a full discussion of Henry's religious position, see G. W. Bernard, *The King's Reformation* (2005).

30. Ibid.

31. Statute 25 Henry VIII, cap.22, *Statutes of the Realm*, III, pp.471–4.

32. Loades, *The Boleyns*, pp.134–5.

33. There is a theory that the foetus was deformed, and on that basis Henry convinced himself that he was not its begetter. However that story can be traced back no further than Nicholas Sanders, writing in the reign of Elizabeth. There is no contemporary evidence to support it. Retha Warnicke, *The Rise and Fall of Anne Boleyn* (1989); E. W. Ives, *The Life and Death of Anne Boleyn* (2004).

34. Witchcraft was not mentioned in the charges against her; it seems to have remained a personal conviction on the king's part, no doubt to explain her long hold over him. Warnicke, *Rise and Fall*, pp.199–233.

35. MacCulloch, *Thomas Cranmer*, p.158; Ives, *Life and Death*, pp.354–6.

36. Loades, *Six Wives*, p.88. Chapuys described her as being 'of medium stature', but to modern eyes she was plain and dumpy.

37. For a full discussion of the circumstances of Mary's surrender, see Loades, *Mary Tudor* (2011), pp.54–8.

38. G. E. Cockayne, *The Complete Peerage*, ed. V. Gibbs (1910–59).

39. Hall, *Chronicle*, p.825.

40. On Henry's constant need for more offspring, see Loades, *Henry VIII, passim.*

41. Loades, *Six Wives*, pp.102–3.

42. Retha Warnicke, *The Marrying of Anne of Cleves* (2000), pp.183–6.

43. Lord Edmund does not even appear upon a commission of the peace until 1524. Lacey Baldwin Smith, *A Tudor Tragedy* (1961), pp.37–45; *Letters and Papers*, IV(i), no. 137.

44. *ODNB.*

45. The queen's confession. *Historical Manuscripts Commission, Bath Papers* II, pp.8 et seq.

46. *Letters and Papers*, XVI, No. 1385.

47. *L & P*, VIII, No.797.

2 The International Scene

1. Memorandum of 31 October 1534; *Letters and Papers*, VII, no 1336.

2. M-J. Rodriguez Salgado, 'The Habsburg-Valois Wars' in *The Reformation, 1520–1559*, Vol. 2 of The New Cambridge Modern History, ed. G. R. Elton (1990), p.387.

3. E. W. Ives, *The Life and Death of Anne Boleyn*, pp. 312–4.

4. David Loades, *Henry VIII*, p.281.

5. 'The Habsburg-Valois Wars', p.388.

6. Loades, *Henry VIII*, p.281.

7. *State Papers*, VIII, p.1; *Letters and Papers*, XII (ii), no. 1004.

8. Scarisbrick, *Henry VIII*, p.356.

9. *Letters and Papers*, XIII, (i), no. 380. The portrait now hangs in the National Gallery.

10. *L & P*, XIII (i), no. 271.

11. *L & P*, XIV, (ii), no. 400. Her words were reported by George Constantine.

12. Scarisbrick, *Henry VIII*, pp.358–9.

13. Wilkins, *Concilia*, III, p.840. There are doubts about how fully the Bull was promulgated, even now.

14. Loades, *The Tudor Navy* (1992), pp.120–1.

15. Ibid.

16. *Spanish Calendar*, VI, p. 33; *L & P*. XIV,(i), no. 36.

17. *L & P*, XIV, (ii), no. 52; Scarisbrick, *Henry VIII*, p.364.

18. *L & P*, XIV, (i), nos. 103, 580.

19. Ibid, no. 981.

20. Retha M. Warnicke, *The Marrying of Anne of Cleves* (2000), pp.12–35.

21. Ibid, p.238.

22. *L & P*, XIV, (i), no. 920.

23. For the circumstances under which this portrait was painted, see Warnicke, *The Marrying*, pp.88–93.

24. *L & P*, XIV, (ii), nos 169, 222, 328; Scarisbrick, *Henry VIII*, p.370.

25. Warnicke, *The Marrying*, pp.75–9; *L & P*, XIV (ii), no. 33.

26. Ibid, pp.119–20. On the relations between the Merchant Adventurers and the Crown, see D. R. Bisson, *The Merchant Adventurers of England* (1993), pp.1–30.

27. TNA SP1/157 ff.126–30; *L & P*, XIV, (ii), no. 677; SP1/155 ff.85–8; *L & P*, XX (ii), no. 992.

28. *L & P*, XIV (ii), no. 258; M. St Clare Byrne, *The Lisle Letters*, (1981) p.470.

29. Hall, *Chronicle*, pp.833 et seq.

30. Scarisbrick, *Henry VIII*, p.370.

31. Ibid, p.371.

32. John Strype, *Ecclesiastical Memorials* (1822), II, p.462.

33. *L & P*, XIV (i), no. 920.

34. *L & P*, XV, (ii), nos 822–3, 861 (2) I.

35. Ibid, no. 850 (3).

36. Wilkins, *Concilia*, III, p.851; *L & P*, XV, nos 908, 930.

37. Warnicke, *Marrying*, p.240.

38. *L & P*, XV, no. 970.

39. *L & P*, XIV, (ii), no. 33.

40. Scarisbrick, *Henry VIII*, pp.375–9.

3 Domestic Politics

1. G. R. Elton, *Thomas Cromwell* (ed. 2008), pp.8–10.

2. Ibid, p.2. Apart from the story of his service in the French army, there is no record of how he lived during these years.

3. R. B. Merriman, *The Life and Letters of Thomas Cromwell* (1902), I, p.5.

4. John Foxe, *Acts and Monuments* (1583), p.1178.

5. *Letters and Papers*, III, nos 2441, 2455, 2557, 3081 etc.

6. P. Gwyn, *The King's Cardinal*, pp.270–77.

7. Wolsey continued as Bishop of Winchester until his death in November 1530.

8. M. J. Kelly, 'The Submission of the Clergy', *Transactions of the Royal Historical Society*, 5th series, XV (1965), p103.

9. G. R. Elton, *The Tudor Constitution* (1982), pp.233–240.

10. Statute 24 Henry VIII, cap.12, *Statutes of the Realm*, III, p.427.

11. Statute 27 Henry VIII, cap.24, *Statutes of the Realm*, III, pp.555–8.

12. M. L. Robertson, 'Thomas Cromwell and west country management', *Historical Journal*, XXXII (1989), pp.793–816.

13. G. R. Elton, *The Tudor Revolution in Government* (1953), pp.133–9.

14. Ibid, pp.189–223.

15. F. C. Dietz, *English Government Finance, 1485–1558* (1964), pp.103–8.

16. Statute 27 Henry VIII, cap.28, *Statutes of the Realm*, III, pp.575–8.

17. G. W. Bernard, 'The Dissolution of the Monasteries', *History*, XC (2011).

18. M. D. Knowles, *The Religious Orders in England*, III, *The Tudor Age* (1959)

19. Scarisbrick, *Henry VIII*, pp.337–8.

20. P. Hughes, *The Reformation in England* (1956), I, pp.65–7.

21. Bernard, 'Dissolution': Hughes, *Reformation*, pp.105–6.

22. Statute 31 Henry VIII, cap.13, *Statutes of the Realm*, III, pp.733–9; P. Cunich, 'The Dissolution' in *Monks of England; the Benedictines in England from Augustine to the Present Day*, ed. D Rees (1997).

23. 'The Lincoln Articles, 9th October 1536', R. W. Hoyle, *The Pilgrimage of Grace and the Politics of the 1530s* (2001), pp.455–6.

24. Ibid, pp.143–55.

25. Ibid, pp.224–7.

26. M. H. and R. Dodds, *The Pilgrimage of Grace, 1536–7 and the Exeter Conspiracy 1538* (2 vols. 1915).

27. M. Bateson, 'Aske's examination', *English Historical Review*, V, 1890, pp. 550–73.

28. 'The Pontefract Articles', Hoyle, *Pilgrimage*, pp.460–3.

29. *L & P*, XII, (i), nos 43–5; 'The manner of the taking of Robert Aske'; Hoyle, *Pilgrimage*, p.368.

30. G. R. Elton, *Policy and Police* (1972), p.387.

31. For an account of Cromwell's part in Mary's rehabilitation, see David Loades, *Mary Tudor: A Life*, pp.102–4.

32. *L & P*, XII (i), no. 1212; (ii), no. 908; XIII (ii), no. 986.

33. Hazel Pierce, *Margaret Pole, Countess of Salisbury, 1473–1541* (2003), p.115.

34. Ibid, pp.115–40.

35. M. L. Bush, 'The Tudors and Royal Race', *History*, LV (1970), pp.37–48; *L & P*, XIII, (ii), nos 802, 961.

36. Pierce, *Margaret Pole*, pp.115, 137, 139, 169, 172.

37. Ibid, pp.177–8.

38. This is the main argument of G. W. Bernard, *The King's Reformation* (2005).

39. W. H. Frere and W. M. Kennedy, *Visitation Articles and Injunctions of the Period of the Reformation* (1910), II, pp.34–43; P. L. Hughes and J. F. Larkin, *Tudor Royal Proclamations* (1964), I, pp.284–6.

40. David Daniell, *The Bible in English; its History and Influence* (2003).

41. David Loades, 'John Foxe and Henry VIII', *The John Foxe Bulletin*, I, (i), 2002, pp.5–12.

42. Scarisbrick, *Henry VIII*, pp.400–1.

43. Diarmaid MacCulloch, *Thomas Cranmer*, pp. 250–2.

44. L. B. Smith, *A Tudor Tragedy* (1961), pp.64–8.

4 The Summer of 1540

1. *L & P*, XV, no. 861; Warnicke, *The Marrying of Anne of Cleves*, p.155.

2. G. Burnet, *History of the Reformation* (1679–1715), I, ii, p.299.

3. Hall, *Chronicle*, pp.302–3. Supper would have been at 4 p.m.

4. Brantome explained 'everyone was eavesdropping, as is the custom'. Pierre de Bourdeille, Seigneur de Brantome, *The Lives of Gallant Ladies*, trans. A. Brown (1960), p.240; Warnicke, *The Marrying…*, p.161.

5. BL MS Cotton Otho C. X, f.247; J. Strype, *Ecclesiastical Memorials* (1720), II, (i), p.461.

6. Burnet, I, (i), p.296; *L & P*, XV, no. 825.

7. Warnicke, *The Marrying…*, pp.166–7.

8. BL MS Royal, App. 89, ff. 104–9.

9. *L & P*, XV, nos 642, 678; Strype, *Memorials*, I, (ii), p.437.

10. This reaction does not seem to have soured relations in the longer term. After Anne's dismissal, the two became firm friends. *Cal. Span.*, VI, (i), pp.143, 149, 161; David Loades, *Mary Tudor: A Life*, pp.116–7.

11. Warnicke, *The Marrying…*, p.175.

12. *State Papers of Henry VIII*, VIII, pp.244, 258–60, 265–76.

13. Warnicke, *The Marrying…*, p.184.

14. Ibid, p.183.

15. BL Ms Cotton Titus B I, f. 409; Strype, II, (i), p.452.

16. D. MacCulloch, *Thomas Cranmer*, pp.273–4.

17. *L & P*, XV, no. 874; XVI, nos 503, 1500; XVII, no. 135; Patrick Carter, 'Financial Administration, Patronage and Profit in Tudor England; the career of Sir Wymond Carew (1498–1549), *Southern History*, 21, 1998; *Cal.Ven.* VI, no. 222, 29 July 1540.

18. *L & P*, XV, no. 801; G. R. Elton, 'Thomas Cromwell's Decline and Fall', *Studies in Tudor and Stuart Politics and Government* (1974), I, p.220.

19. MacCulloch, *Cranmer*, pp.161–6; Frere and Kennedy, *Visitation Articles and Injunctions*, II, pp.1–11.

20. *State Papers*, I, p.605; Scarsibrick, *Henry VIII*, pp.369–70.

21. Elton, 'Thomas Cromwell's Decline and Fall', pp.209–10.

22. Rory McEntegart, *Henry VIII, the League of Schmalkalden, and the English Reformation* (2002), pp.27–33, 35–8.

23. A. J. Slavin, 'Cromwell, Cranmer and Lord Lisle; a study in the politics of Reform', *Albion*, 9, 1977, pp.316–36.

24. *Lords Journals*, I, pp128–9. This speech, although delivered in English, is preserved only in a Latin version.

25. *ODNB: The Complete Peerage*.

26. Marillac to Francis I, 1st June 1540; *L & P*, XV, no. 736.

27. Elton, 'Thomas Cromwell's Decline and Fall', p.219.

28. Ibid, pp.221–2.

29. R. B. Merriman, *Life and Letters of Thomas Cromwell*, (1902), II, p.266.

30. Burnet, *History of the Reformation*, IV, p.415 et seq.

31. Ibid.

32. Merriman, *Life and Letters*, II, p.273.

33. Elton, 'Decline and Fall', p.228.

34. Hall, *Chronicle*, p.838.

35. Scarisbrick, *Henry VIII*, p.427. This was in the spring of 1541, when he was in pain from his ulcerated leg, and disposed to complain about everything, including his council. He began, as he said, to 'smell the truth' about Cromwell's fall, and how he had been misled.

36. *L & P*, XV, no. 613 (12); XVI, nos 1385, 1409; TNA E101/422/15.

37. Warnicke, *The Marrying…*, pp.184–5.

38. L. B. Smith, *A Tudor Tragedy*, p.123; Luis Vives, *The office and dutie of an husband* (London, 1553), Vol. 2. The story is told that on a visit to his son, he called Catherine before him, and when she knelt he said 'Catherine from now on I want you never to do that again, but rather that all these ladies and my whole kingdom should bend the knee to you, for I wish to make you queen'. However, as far as the records go, this is mere fiction. M. A. S Hume, *Chronicle of Henry VIII*, (1889), pp.75–6; Nicholas Harpesfield, *A treatise on the pretended divorce between Henry VIII and Catherine of Aragon*, ed. N. Pocock (Camden Society, 1878) p.263.

39. Hall, *Chronicle*, II, p.310.

40. L. B. Smith, *A Tudor Tragedy*, pp.125–6.

5 The Royal Bride

1. *L & P*, XI, no. 285; XIII, (i), no. 995.

2. William Thomas, *The Pilgrim, a Dialogue on the Life and Actions of King Henry VIII*, ed. J. A. Froude (1861), p.157; Smith, *A Tudor Tragedy*, p.146.

3. Hume, *Chronicle of Henry VIII*, p.77.

4. *L & P*, XV, no. 21 (where it is identified incorrectly as the household of Anne of Cleves). The queen would not have been personally involved in the appointment of menial servants.

5. Smith, *A Tudor Tragedy*, p.148.

6. *L & P*, XVI, no. 1389.

7. Ibid, no. 804. Accounts for the 6th May 1541.

8. *L & P*, XVI, no.316.

9. Ibid, no. 12.

10. Smith, *A Tudor Tragedy*, p.149.

11. *L & P*, XV, no. 901; XVI, no. 12.

12. Warnicke, *The Marrying*, p.246.

13. *State Papers*, I, pp.714, 716; Warnicke, pp.248–9.

14. *L & P*, XVI, no. 436. Chapuys to the Queen of Hungary, 8 January 1541.

15. Ibid, no.314.

16. *L & P*, XVI, no. 142; Marillac to Montmorency, 11 October 1540.

17. Every time that the king changed his residence, a massive removal operation had to be carried out, because all the trappings of royalty had to move with him.

18. *L & P*, XVI, no. 589.

19. Smith, *Tudor Tragedy*, p.152.

20. *L & P*, XVI, no. 835.

21. Ibid, no. 712. Marillac to Montmorency, 10 April 1541.

22. Smith, *Tudor Tragedy*, p.155.

23. *L & P*, XVI, no. 1317.

24. Smith, p.156.

25. *L & P*, XVI, no. 1320.

26. Ibid, no. 467.

27. Ibid, no. 101.

28. The duchess was clearly interested primarily in getting her ward into the royal bed. She would therefore not have disclosed any information (or suspicion) which she might have had. Burnet, *History of the Reformation*, IV, p.504.

29. *L & P*, XVI, nos 1385, 1416.

30. Ibid, no. 159. Culpepper's confession.

31. An Act whereby divers offences be made High Treason. Statute 26 Henry VIII, cap.13. *Statutes of the Realm*, III, pp.508–9.

32. It is not known when the duchess visited the court, but the Christmas festivities would be a reasonable pretext. Catherine is alleged to have said 'my lady of Norfolk hath desired me to be good unto him, and so I will'. *L & P*, XVI, no. 1416 (2).

33. TNA SP1/167, f. 161. Robert Davenport's confession.

34. Ibid.

35. Scarisbrick, *Henry VIII*, pp.380–1.

36. Foxe, *Acts and Monuments*.

37. Scarisbrick, p.382.

38. Bernard, *The King's Reformation*, pp 574–5.

39. *L & P*, XV, no. 136.

40. Gordon Donaldson, *Scotland; James V to VII* (1979); David Head, 'Henry VIII's Scottish Policy; a reassessment', *Scottish*

Historical Review, 61, 1982.

41. James did not present any reasons for his non-appearance, which annoyed Henry still more.

6 The Progress of 1541

1. *L & P*, XVI, nos 868, 941, 1130, 1183.

2. Scarisbrick, *Henry VIII*, p.427.

3. Smith, *Tudor Tragedy*, p.175.

4. *L & P*, XVI, no. 903.

5. Ibid. nos 1088–9.

6. Smith, pp.176–7. Norfolk had been responsible for the accommodation of the travelling court, but not for arranging the entertainments. They would have been under the control of the Master of the Revels.

7. *L & P*, XVI, no. 1126.

8. Edward Hall, *Henry VIII* (taken from the *Chronicle*), ed. C. Whibley (1904), II, p.313.

9. *L & P*, XVI, nos 1183, 1297; Scarisbrick, p.428.

10. Culpepper was a man with a criminal past, because he had recently been pardoned by the king for raping a park keeper's wife, with aggravated violence. Catherine seems to have been unaware of this. Julia Fox, *Jane Boleyn* (2007), pp. 287–8.

11. The game of courtly love was essentially platonic, consisting mainly in the exchange of tokens. The gallant pretended to love his lady, but was not supposed to become romantically involved. David Loades, *The Tudor Court* (1986), pp.11–2.

12. TNA SP1/167 f157. Culpepper's confession.

13. Fox, *Jane Boleyn*, p. 293.

14. TNA SP1/167, f149. Katherine Tylney's confession.

15. Ibid, ff. 159–60. Jane Rochford's confession.

16. *L & P*, XVI, no. 1139.

17. Fox, *Jane Boleyn*, pp.295–6.

18. *L & P*, XVI, no. 1134.

19. TNA SP1/167, f 157.

20. B. Harris, *Aristocratic Women, 1450–1550; Marriage and Family, Property and Careers* (2002), pp.32–42; *ODNB*.

21. *L & P*, III, (ii), no. 1522; Hall, *Henry VIII*, I, pp.238–40.

22. Fox, *Jane Boleyn*, p.35.

23. *ODNB*; Gwyn, *The King's Cardinal*.

24. J. Rowley Williams, *Jane Boleyn, Viscountess Rochford* (2012).

25. There is some evidence that she had fallen out with Anne by 1535, when her name has been linked to a demonstration in favour of Princess Mary, but that depends upon a marginal note by the Bishop of Tarbes. Rowley Williams, *Jane Boleyn*.

26. *ODNB*; David Loades, *The Boleyns*, p.140.

27. Fox, *Jane Boleyn*, p.182.

28. Elton, 'Thomas Cromwell's Decline and Fall,' pp.210–14.

29. Loades, *The Boleyns*, pp.162–4.

30. *The Life of Cardinal Wolsey by George Cavendish*, ed. S. W. Singer (1827), pp.451–3; Ives, *Life and Death of Anne Boleyn*, p.325.

31. Ives, *Life and Death*, p.331; Fox, *Jane Boleyn*, p.352.

32. Ibid, p.247–52.

33. BL Cotton MS, Vespasian F.XIII, f.199; *L & P*, X., no. 1010.

34. The only role for a noblewoman in the court (apart from that of visitor) was as a lady of the Privy Chamber to a queen.

35. *L & P*, X, nos 926, 1000; Loades, *Tudor Queens of England*, p.131.

36. Loades, *Mary Tudor; A Life*, pp.103–8.

37. Fox, *Jane Boleyn*, p.226.

38. Hall, *Chronicle*, p.825.

39. *L & P*, XI, no. 17.

40. An Act for My Lady Rochford's jointure. 31 Henry VIII, cap. 20. Not printed in *Statutes of the Realm*.

41. Hazel Pierce, *Margaret Pole*, pp.115–40.

42. For a discussion of these diplomatic initiatives, see Scarisbrick, *Henry VIII*, pp.365–9.

43. Fox, *Jane Boleyn*, p.258.

44. Ibid, pp.269–70.

45. See Catherine's confession. *Historical Manuscripts Commission Reports*, Bath Papers, Vol. II (1907), pp.8–10.

7 Adultery Detected

1. *L & P*, XVI, no. 101.

2. Smith, *Tudor Tragedy*, pp.158–9.

3. Loades, *Henry VIII*, p.294; H. Nicholas, *Proceedings and Ordinances of the Privy Council of England* (1837), VII, pp.352–4.

4. *L & P*, XVI, no. 1320. 5 November 1541.

5. Ibid, no. 1321. Examination of Henry Mannox, 5 November 1541.

6. Fox, *Jane Boleyn*, pp.283–5; *Proceedings and Ordinances*, VII, pp.354–5.

7. *L & P*, XVI, nos 1328, 1332.

8. Ibid, no. 1426; *Proceedings and Ordinances*, VII, p.355.

9. *Cal. Span.* VI, (i), pp.211, 411.

10. *State Papers of Henry VIII*, II, p.691.

11. *Miscellaneous Writings of Thomas Cranmer*, ed. J. C. Cox (Parker Society, 1846), p.406.

12. Ibid, pp.408–9. On the issue of pre-contact, see Fox, *Jane Boleyn*, pp.284–6.

13. Smith, *Tudor Tragedy*, pp.183–4.

14. *HMC*, Bath Papers, II, pp.8–9.

15. *L & P*, XVII, Appendix B, no. 4.

16. Ibid.

17. *L & P*, XVI, no. 1337. Examination of Katheryn Tylney, 13 November 1541.

18. Ibid, no. 1332.

19. Ibid, no. 1331. 'The Queen's departing for Syon shall be on Monday next.'

20. *HMC*, Bath Papers, II, pp.9–10.

21. Ibid, p.9.

22. The Confession of Margaret Morton to Sir Anthony Browne. *L & P*, XVI, no. 1338.

23. Fox, *Jane Boleyn*, pp.295–6.

24. Ibid.

25. Culpepper's deposition, TNA SP1/167 ff.157–9.

26. Statute 26 Henry VIII, cap. 13, *Statutes of the Realm*, III, pp.508–9.

27. G. R. Elton, *The Tudor Constitution*, pp.59–61.

28. *State Papers*, I, (ii), p.707.

29. Southampton and Wriothesley to Ralph Sadler, 21 December 1541; *L & P*, XVI, no. 1467.

30. Chapuys to Charles V, 25 March 1542. *L & P*, XVII, no. 197. See also, ibid, no. 714 (23).

31. Fox, *Jane Boleyn*, pp.302–3.

32. *Cal. Span.*, VI, (i), no. 228.

33. *L & P*, XVI, no. 1401.

34. *Lord Journals*, I, p.165.

35. Ibid, I, p.168. Saturday, 21 January 1541/2.

36. Ibid, p.171. Saturday, 28 January.

37. Ibid, p.175.

38. Statute 33 Henry VIII, cap.21, *Statutes of the Realm*, III, p.859.

39. Ibid.

40. Smith, *Tudor Tragedy*, p.202.

41. *Lords Journals*, I, p.171.

42. Smith, *Tudor Tragedy*, p.204.

8 The End of Catherine

1. Fox, *Jane Boleyn*, p.304.

2. The chronicle of Anthony Anthony is now lost, but notes on his account of the trial of Anne Boleyn are bound into Thomas Turner's copy of Lord Herbert of Cherbury's *Life and Rainge of King Henry the Eighth*, now Bodleian Folio Delta 624, pp. 381–5. The chronicle itself was used by Burnet in his *History of the Reformation*.

3. *Cal. Span.* VI, (i), no. 232.

4. Otwell Johnson's manuscript survives as TNA SP1/169 no. 32.

5. *L & P*, XVII, no. 100.

6. TNA SP1/169, no. 32.

7. Fox, *Jane Boleyn*, pp.310–11.

8. None of the accounts, eye-witness or otherwise, make any reference to her recent bouts of hysteria, which were presumably not considered relevant.

9. *L & P*, XVII, nos 124, 178 and appendix B, no. 13.

10. *State Papers*, I, p.696; Warnicke, *The Marrying of Anne of Cleves*, p.250.

11. *Statutes of the Realm*, IV, (i), p.857; *L & P*, XVII, no. 28 and appendix B, no. 48.

12. Chapuys to Charles V, 25 March 1542; *L & P*, XVII, no. 197.

13. Ibid, no. 283

14. For a full discussion of Morley's translation of *Boccaccio* and its significance, see Fox, *Jane Boleyn*, pp.312–14.

15. Ibid.

16. Essex Record Office MS DP/27/5/1, f.31.

17. *Lords' Journals*, I, p.171; Smith, *Tudor Tragedy*, p.202.

18. *L & P*, XIX, no. 741. For Henry's enthusiasm for the campaign, see Scarisbrick, *Henry VIII*, p.447.

19. *L & P*, XIX, nos. 955–6.

20. Ibid, (ii), no. 424, appendix 10.

21. Nicholas Wotton's despatches about the Franco–Imperial negotiations. *L & P*, XIX, (ii), nos 267–8.

22. *State Papers*, X, p.104.

23. Margaret Rule, *The Mary Rose* (1982), pp.13–38; Peter Marsden ed., *Mary Rose: Your Noblest Shippe* (2009), pp.1–12.

24. Boulogne was to be returned to France in eight years time, on payment of 2 million crowns. Scarisbrick, Henry VIII, p.464.

25. Chapuys to the Queen of Hungary, 10 November 1541. *Cal. Span.* VI, (i), p.384.

26. Fox, *Jane Boleyn, passim*.

27. 'If any person or persons … do maliciously wish or desire by words or writing, or by craft imagine, invent, practise or attempt any bodily harm to be done or committed to the king's most royal person, the queen's or the heir's apparent … being thereof lawfully convicted according to the laws and customs of this realm, shall be adjudged traitors. *Statutes of the Realm*, III, p.509.

9 Epilogue

1. N. S. Tjernagel, *Henry VIII and the Lutherans* (1965), 230; *L & P*, XVI, no. 271.

2. Hughes and Larkin, *Tudor Royal Proclamations*, I, p.301.

3. MacCulloch, *Thomas Cranmer*, pp.295–323.

4. *L & P*, XVII, no. 63.

5. Ibid, nos 441, 447.

6. Ibid, no. 661

7. Ibid, nos 994, 996, 998.

8. Scarisbrick, *Henry VIII*, p.435; *L & P*, XVII, no. 1016.

9. David Loades, *Henry VIII*, pp.300; Gervase Phillips, *The Anglo-Scottish Wars; a Military History* (1999), pp.150–53.

10. *L & P*, XVIII, (i), no. 44.

11. Ten of the prisoners who were considered the most trustworthy also swore to a secret article that Henry himself would receive the Scottish crown if Mary died. *L & P*, XVIII, nos 7, 22, 44.

12. Scarisbrick, p.437.

13. *L & P*, XVIII, nos 139, 155, 188–9.

14. Ibid, (i), no. 425.

15. On the politics of Scotland at this time, see G. Donaldson, *Scotland, James V to James VII* (1965); D. M Head, 'Henry VIII's Scottish Policy', *Scottish Historical Review*, 61, 1982, pp.1–24.

16. *L & P*, XVIII, no. 804.

17. Ibid, (ii), nos 128, 132.

18. Loades, *Henry VIII*, p.300.

19. *L & P*, XIX, (i), nos 33, 51, 58.

20. *State Papers*, V, pp.363–5, 386 et seq.

21. D. Loades and C. S. Knighton, 'Lord Admiral Lisle and the Invasion of Scotland, 1544', *Naval Miscellany*, VII, ed. S Rose (2008), pp.57–96.

22. Ibid, p.63; Sir J. Balfour Paul, 'Edinburgh in 1544 and Hertford's Invasion', *Scottish Historical Review*, 8, 1910–11, pp.113–31.

23. Privy Council to Hertford and Lisle, 15 May 1544; Loades and

Knighton, pp.92–3.

24. *L & P*, XIX, (i), no. 714.

25. Ibid, (ii), no. 304.

26. Loades, *The Six Wives of Henry VIII*, pp.132–3; Susan James, *Catherine Parr; Henry VIII's Last Love* (2008).

27. Loades, *Six Wives*, p.133.

28. Ibid, p.134.

29. Statute 35 Henry VIII, cap.1, *Statutes of the Realm*, III, p.955.

30. Scarisbrick, p.457.

31. Loades, *Six Wives*, p.135.

32. Foxe, *Acts and Monuments* (1583), pp. 1242–4.

33. Ibid; Scarisbrick, p.479.

34. Foxe, *Acts and Monuments* (1583), pp. 1242–4.

35. Loades, *Henry VIII*, pp.299–325.

36. Elton, *The Tudor Constitution*, pp.59–79.

37. Scarisbrick, *Henry VIII*, p.450.

38. Conyers Read, *Mr Secretary Cecil and Queen Elizabeth* (1955), p.122

Bibliography

Manuscripts:

The National Archive: SP1/155, 157, 167, 169.

The British Library: MS Royal, Appendix.

MS Cotton Titus B.I.

MS Cotton Vespasian F.XIII.

The Bodleian Library: Folio Delta 624.

Printed Sources:

Bourdeille, Pierre de, Sieur de Brantome, *The Lives of Gallant Ladies*, trs. A Brown (1960).

Byrne, M. St. Clare, *The Lisle Letters* (1981).

Calendar of State Papers, Venetian, ed. by Rawdon Brown *et al.* (1864–98).

Calendar of State Papers, Spanish, ed. Royall Tyler *et al.* (1862–1954).

Certain Sermons or Homilies Appointed by the King… (1547).

Cockayne, G. E., *The Complete Peerage*, ed. V. Gibbs (1910–59).

Foxe, John, *The Acts and Monuments of the English Martyrs* (1583).

Frere, W. H. and W. M. Kennedy, *Visitation Articles and Injunction of the period of the Reformation* (1910).

Hall, Edward, *Chronicle* (ed. 1809).

Historical Manuscripts Commission, Bath Papers, II (1904–8).

Hume, M. A. S., ed., *Chronicle of Henry VIII* (1889).

Letters and Papers… of the Reign of Henry VIII, ed. J. S. Brewer *et al.* (1862–1932).

Loades, D. and C. S. Knighton, 'Lord Admiral Lisle and the Invasion of Scotland, 1544' in *Naval Miscellany*, Vol. VII, ed. S Rose (2008).

Lords' Journals (1846).

Miscellaneous Writings of Thomas Cranmer, ed. J. C. Cox (Parker Society, 1846).

Nicholas, N. H., *Proceedings and Ordinances of the Privy Council of England* (1837).

Original Letters Relative to the English Reformation, ed. H. Robinson (Parker Society, 1846–7).

Rotuli Parliamentorum, ed. J. Strachey *et al.* 6 vols (1767–77),

The Life and Death of Cardinal Wolsey by George Cavendish ed. S. W. Singer, (1827).

State Papers of Henry VIII (1830–52).

Statutes of the Realm, ed. A Luders *et al.* (1810–28).

Thomas, William,*The Pilgrim: a Dialogue on the Life and Actions of King Henry VIII*, ed. J. A. Froude (1861).

Vives, Luis, *The Office and Duty of an Husband* (1553).

Wilkins, D. *Concilia…* (1737).

Secondary Works:

Anglo, S., *Spectacle, Pageantry and Early Tudor Policy* (1969).

Bateson, M., 'Aske's Examination', *English Historical Review*, 5 (1890).

Bedouelle, Guy and Patrick Le Gal, *Le 'Divorce' du Roi Henri VIII* (1987).

Bisson, D. R., *The Merchant Adventurers of England* (1993).

Bernard, G. W., *The King's Reformation* (2005).

Bernard, G. W., 'The Dissolution of the Monasteries', *History*, 90 (2011).

Burnet, G., *History of the Reformation in England*, ed. N. Pocock (1865).

Bush, M. L., 'The Tudors and the Royal Race', *History*, 55 (1970).

Carter, P., 'Financial Administration; Patronage and Profit in Tudor England; the Career of Sir Wymond Carew', *Southern History*, 21 (1998).

Cavill, P. R., *The English Parliaments of Henry VII* (2009).

Chrimes, S. B., *Henry VII* (1972).

Cunich, P., 'The Dissolution' in *Monks of England: the Benedictines in England from Augustine to the Present Day*, ed. D. Rees (1997).

Daniell, David, *The Bible in English: its History and Influence* (2003).

Dickens, A. G., *The English Reformation* (1964).

Dietz, F. C., *English Government Finance, 1485–1558* (1964).

Dodds, M. H. and R., *The Pilgrimage of Grace, 1536–7, and the Exeter Conspiracy, 1538*, 2 vols (1915).

Donaldson, G., *Scotland: James V to James VII* (1979).

Elton, G. R., *The Tudor Revolution in Government* (1953).

Elton, G. R., *Policy and Police* (1972).

Elton, G. R., 'Thomas Cromwell's Decline and Fall', in *Studies in Tudor and Stuart Politics and Government*, I (1974).

Elton, G. R., *The Tudor Consitution* (1982).

Elton, G. R., *Thomas Cromwell*, ed. D. Loades (2008).

Fox, Julia, *Jane Boleyn* (2007).

Fraser, Antonia, *The Six Wives of Henry VIII* (1993).

Gwyn, Peter, *The King's Cardinal* (1990).

Harris, Barbara, *Edward Stafford, Third Duke of Buckingham* (1986).

Harris, B., *Aristocratic Women, 1450–1550: Marriage and Family, Property and Careers* (2002).

Head, David, 'Henry VIII's Scottish policy: a Reassessment', *Scottish Historical Review*, 61, (1982).

Hoyle, R. W., *The Pilgrimage of Grace and the Politics of the 1530s* (2001).

Hughes, P., *The Reformation in England* (1956).

Ives, E. W., *The Life and Death of Anne Boleyn* (2004).

James, Susan, *Catherine Parr; Henry VIII's Last Love* (2008).

Kelly, H. A., *The Matrimonial Trials of Henry VIII* (1976).

Kelly, M. J., 'The Submission of the Clergy', *Transactions of the Royal Historical Society*, 15 (1965).

Knecht, R. J., *Francis I* (1982).

Knowles, M. D., *The Religious Orders in England III, The Tudor Age* (1959).

Loades, David, *The Tudor Court* (1986).

Loades, David, *Mary Tudor: A Life* (1989).

Loades, David, *The Tudor Navy* (1992).

Loades, David, 'John Foxe and Henry VIII', *John Foxe Bulletin*, I (i) (2002).

Loades, David, *The Tudor Queens of England* (2009).

Loades, David, *The Six Wives of Henry VIII* (2009).

Loades, David, *Henry VIII* (2011).

Loades, David, *The Boleyns* (2011).

Loades, David, *Mary Tudor* (2011).

MacCulloch, D., *Thomas Cranmer* (1996).

Marsden, Peter, ed., *Mary Rose: Your Noblest Shippe* (2009).

Mattingly, Garrett. *Catherine of Aragon* (1963).

McEntegart, Rory, *Henry VIII, the League of Schmalkalden and the English Reformation* (2002).

Merriman, R. B., *The Life and Letters of Thomas Cromwell* (1902).

Miller, Helen, *Henry VIII and the English Nobility* (1986).

Murphy, B., *Bastard Prince: Henry VIII's Lost Son* (2001).

Nicholson, G., 'The Act of Appeals and the English Reformation' in *Law and Government under the Tudors*, ed. C. Cross *et al.* (1988).

Oxford Dictionary of National Biography (2005).

Paul, Sir J. Balfour, 'Edinburgh in 1544 and Hertford's Invasion', *Scottish Historical Review*, 8 (1910–11).

Phillips, Gervase, *The Anglo-Scottish Wars, 1513–1550; a Military History* (1999).

Pierce, Hazel, *Margaret Pole, Countess of Salisbury, 1473–1541* (2003).

Reed, Conyers, *Mr Secretary Cecil and Queen Elizabeth* (1955).

Robertson, M. L., 'Thomas Cromwell and West Country Management', *Historical Journal*, 32 (1989).

Rodriguez Salgado, M-J., 'The Habsburg Valois Wars' in *The Reformation, 1520–1559*, Vol. 2 of the *New Cambridge Modern History*, ed. G. R. Elton (1992).

Rowley Williams, J., *Jane Boleyn, Viscountess Rochford* (2012).

Rule, Margaret, *The Mary Rose* (1982).

Scarisbrick, J., *Henry VIII* (1968).

Slavin, A. J., 'Cromwell, Cranmer and Lord Lisle; a study in the Politics of Reform', *Albion*, 9 (1977).

Smith, L. B. *A Tudor Tragedy* (1961).

Strype, J., *Ecclesiastical Memorials* (ed. 1822).

Tjernagel, N. S., *Henry VIII and the Lutherans* (1965).

Warnicke, Retha, *The Rise and Fall of Anne Boleyn* (1989).

Warnicke, Retha, *The Marrying of Anne of Cleves* (2000).

Wood, M. A., *Letters of Royal and Illustrious Ladies*, 3 vols, (1846).

List of Illustrations

1. Courtesy of Elizabeth Norton.
2. Courtesy of Elizabeth Norton.
3. Courtesy of Ripon Cathedral.
4. Courtesy of Ripon Cathedral.
5. Courtesy of Elizabeth Norton.
6. Courtesy of Elizabeth Norton.
7. Courtesy of Stephen Porter.
8. Courtesy of Elizabeth Norton.
9. Courtesy of Amberley Archive
10. Courtesy of Jonathan Reeve JR1001b66fp100 15001550.
11. Courtesy of Jonathan Reeve JR1169b2p7 15001550.
12. Courtesy of Jonathan Reeve JR1174b2p87 15001550.
13. Courtesy of Elizabeth Norton.
14. Courtesy of Elizabeth Norton.
15. Courtesy of Jonathan Reeve JR896b7p161 15001550.
16. Courtesy of Jonathan Reeve JRCD3b20p913 15001550.
17. Courtesy of Jonathan Reeve JRCD2b20p769 15001550.
18. Courtesy of Elizabeth Norton.
19. Courtesy of Jonathan Reeve JR1018b5fp204 15001550.
20. Courtesy of Jonathan Reeve JR1091b20p884 15001550.
21. Courtesy of Jonathan Reeve JR735b46fp186 14501500.
22. Courtesy of Elizabeth Norton.
23. Courtesy of Jonathan Reeve JR1151b66p1 15001550.
24. Courtesy of Jonathan Reeve JR1177b2p167B 15001550.
25. Courtesy of Jonathan Reeve JR1172b2p57T 15001550.
26. Courtesy of Stephen Porter.
27. Courtesy of Elizabeth Norton.

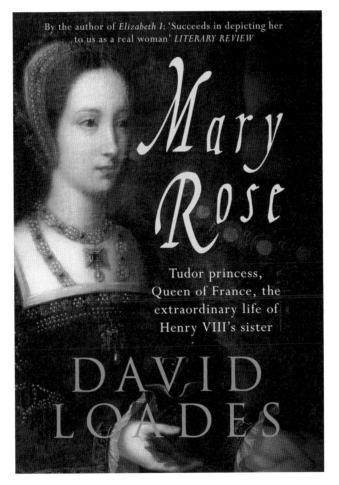

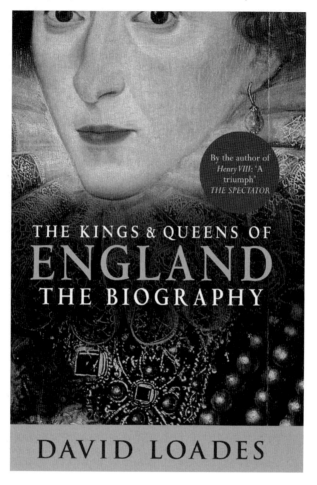

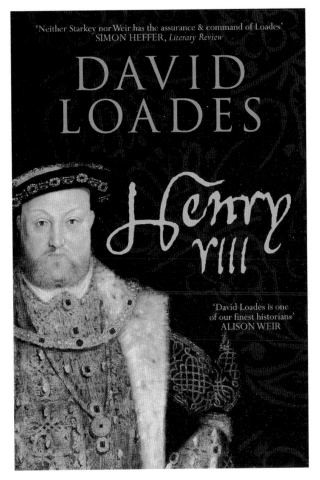

Index